DeFord Bailey

DeFord Bailey:
A Black Star
in Early Country Music

David C. Morton
with Charles K. Wolfe

Country Music Foundation Press
Nashville, Tennessee

Cloth: 1st printing, 1991.
Paper: 1st printing, 1991; 2nd printing, 1993.
Revised paperback edition: 2023.

Frontispiece: Bailey in the 1970s. Photograph by Marilyn K. Morton.

ISBN: 978-0-915608-39-3

The Library of Congress has cataloged the 1991 hardcover and paperback editions
as follows:

Morton, David C., 1945-
    DeFord Bailey: a Black star in early country music / David C. Morton
with Charles K. Wolfe
    p. cm.
    Includes bibliographical references and index.
    ISBN 0-87049-698-0 (cloth: alk. paper)
    ISBN 0-87049-792-8 (pbk.: alk. paper)
    1. Bailey, DeFord. 2. Country musicians—Biography.   I. Wolfe,
Charles K.   II. Title.
    ML419.B12M7   1991
    788.8'21642'092   dc20
    [B]

                                                    90-22519   CIP
                                                                MN

For Junior, Dezoral, and Christine

I didn't hang 'round.
I came to perform;

Then I went home.

—DeFord Bailey,
inducted into the
Country Music
Hall of Fame, 2005

Contents

Illustrations

Foreword

I was born in August 1982, almost two months after DeFord Bailey's death that July. I didn't learn about DeFord right away, but I inherited my father's love of country music. In the early 2000s, while in college, I began to read books about country music. Even though I saw DeFord Bailey mentioned, I could never find a CD of his music.

Since this was a time before streaming, I would compile homemade CDs from tracks of DeFord that I could find on various blues and country music compilations. Years later, I eventually got a copy of the Tennessee Folklore Society's CD *The Legendary DeFord Bailey: Country Music's First Black Star.*

While there are many 78-rpm records of other solo harmonica players, the distinctive sound of DeFord's homemade harmonica megaphone sent shockwaves through the South, inspiring a whole generation of harmonica players from Sonny Terry to Sonny Boy Williamson I and II. While I had enjoyed DeFord's harmonica playing, my mind was blown to find that he was also a multi-instrumentalist. His playing of left-handed five-string banjo and guitar was a revelation, allowing me to view him as a musician not limited to the harmonica. It was from the Tennessee Folklore Society CD's bibliography that I learned about this very book, *DeFord Bailey: A Black Star in Early Country Music.*

I often recommend this biography so people can understand the complexities of being a Black performer in country music. Through David Morton and Charles K. Wolfe's masterful and thoughtful storytelling, we learn that DeFord's story is in part an introduction to the rural Black stringband traditions of the South and the ways these traditions evolved at the turn of the twentieth century. The story follows the evolution of American music when ragtime, jazz, blues, country, and pop all came into their own. It is also a tale of racism, mistrust, sleight of hand, and many of the most unpleasant parts of the music industry. In reading this book, you will see that in spite of his race and physical handicap, DeFord Bailey found the good in people and continued to let his personal strength, fresh-pressed suit, and trusty harmonica transcend it all.

DeFord certainly inspired me. My first appearances on the Grand Ole Opry in 2008 with the Carolina Chocolate Drops—the first all-Black stringband to appear in the program's history—were driven by my desire to bring the music of DeFord and Black country stringbands back to WSM radio. The Carolina Chocolate Drops had formed in 2005, the same year DeFord was inducted into the Country Music Hall of Fame, and I'll never forget the night we made our debut on the Opry and Marty Stuart joined us on stage playing mandolin on "Sourwood Mountain."

We had been invited to perform on the show by George Hamilton IV, who had seen us at MerleFest. That night, Hamilton came to our guest dressing room and asked if we didn't mind switching dressing rooms with him. His usual room was the Roy Acuff Room, Dressing Room Number One, the top spot at the Opry—and he wanted us to have it. While we were still reveling in the moment, Little Jimmy Dickens, who was celebrating his sixtieth year on the Opry that year, came by and did a buck dance to a few numbers and told me how much he loved the "old-time music" we made.

After the show, our band met in the Porter Wagoner Room with Marty Stuart. He told us that our performance was a "healing moment" for the Opry. Without belaboring the point, he acknowledged that in the past the Opry had been on the wrong side of history when it comes to race, but now it was trying to forge a new path. It was good to hear that from him.

It remains a thrill to perform at the Grand Ole Opry. The best part for me is getting a chance to play a harmonica number for the crowd and hearing the thundering applause that follows the last note. The Grand Ole Opry is one of the greatest shows an artist can play. The excitement for me also comes from knowing that I am highlighting and continuing the legacy of the Harmonica Wizard himself, DeFord Bailey.

Over the years, I have paid my respects to DeFord by visiting the historical markers that can be found in Carthage, Tennessee, and Nashville, playing a little medley of classic DeFord Bailey tunes like "Fox Chase" and "Old Hen Cackle" in tribute to his artistry.

Now, I carry the power of his music in my playing while traveling the world, and I evoke musicians forgotten by time and make them live again. Grand Ole Opry announcer Eddie Stubbs once told me, "Dom, you're the real deal." When the real deal includes DeFord Bailey, that's more than good enough for me. Thank you to the Country Music Hall of Fame and Museum and University of Illinois Press for giving this wonderful autobiography a new life so that DeFord Bailey can continue to "let her go."

Dom Flemons
The American Songster

Acknowledgments

As I indicated by dedicating this book to them, DeFord's children - Junior, Dezoral, and Christine—deserve primary recognition for making this book possible. They assisted and encouraged me throughout the long period it was being prepared and have, in many ways, treated me as a part of their family. They, and other family members including Mrs. Blossie Buford, Mrs. Ida Lee Haynes, and Mr. and Mrs. Haney Rucks, shared numerous memories of DeFord with me. I am indebted to several of DeFord's Opry contemporaries and friends who allowed me to interview them, including Mr. and Mrs. Herman Crook, Alcyone Bate Beasley, Sid Harkreader, Roy Acuff, Sam and Kirk McGee, Vito Pellettieri, Pete (Oswald) Kirby, Howard (Howdy) Forrester, Jud Collins, Bill Monroe, and Zeke Clements. Invaluable assistance with photographs or other materials came from photographers Alan Mayor, Clark Thomas, Dennis Wile, Jimmy Ellis, Dale Ernsberger, and Archie E. Allen; WSM's Jerry Strobel and Les Leverett; staff persons at the Country Music Foundation, Bob Pinson, Charlie Seamann, Ronnie Pugh, and Alan Stoker; CSX Transportation; and Nashville Mayor Richard Fulton. Two close friends, both retired Nashville school teachers, Miss Annie Ruth Stroud and Mrs. G. B. Thackston, assisted me with my first draft of this manuscript. My parents, Mr. and Mrs. Charles W. Morton, who became especially fond of DeFord and visited him often, strongly encouraged me in the preparation of this book. My thanks go to the following people at the Metropolitan Development and Housing Agency (formerly the Nashville Housing Authority): Frances Douglas, Bob Howard, Patricia Gray, Gerald Nicely, and Rayburn Ray. Texas friends who helped in various ways were Mr.

and Mrs. Jack D. Herrington, Sheryl McGuire, Johnnie Griffin, Wanda Roland, Bill Perkins, and artist Rodney Dobbs. Nashville friends who contributed advice and assistance were Tom Ingram, James Talley, Hazel Ferguson, Councilman Mansfield Douglas, Claude Reinhart, Elnora Moore, Bonnie and Bill Myers, and Mr. and Mrs. Morgan Smith. Author Peter Guralnick gave me much encouragement. Others who aided in the preparation of this work were G. Miller Watkins, Orville Nugent, Howard Redmond, Willis Patton, Doc Field of KAT Family Public Relations, Dr. Richard Peterson, and Mary Flannigan.

DeFord attended my wedding in 1976, and my wife, Marilyn K. Morton, has been supportive of my efforts throughout the years of our marriage. She also took some of the photographs of DeFord that have been included in this work.

During the lengthy period I've worked on this biography, I've thought often of my major professor at Vanderbilt University, Frederick Schneider. He was keenly disappointed that, after passing my comprehensive examinations for the Ph.D. in history, I withdrew as a candidate to work full-time for the Housing Authority. In many ways this book is a fulfillment of that uncompleted effort.

Even after long years of research and preparation of a manuscript, this biography might never have occurred without the assistance of Dr. Charles K. Wolfe. His outstanding credentials added credibility to my work and helped to convince the University of Tennessee Press to publish the biography. His editing of my copy and his addition of major sections based on his wide knowledge of the period have made this a book of which we are both quite proud. I owe him a great deal.

—David C. Morton

A number of friends and colleagues have shared memories and research information about DeFord, his music, his times, and his traditions. I would like to single out the following for special thanks. Dick Hulan went far out of his way to provide material about Nashville in the 1960s, and of DeFord's involvement in the folk revival. Sam and Kirk McGee, Ramsey Macon, Sid Harkreader, Katherine Thompson, Alcyone Bate Beasley, Bill Monroe, Ed Shea, Herman Crook, John Hartford, Lewis Crook, Brownie McGhee, Mack Sievers, Omer Forster, Louise and Sophie Tipton, Blythe Poteet, Red Phillips, Eston Macon, Perry Bechtel, Jimmie Riddle, Sally Smith, and Jack Jackson are among the musicians and early Opry members who talked with me about DeFord over the years. Other researchers in blues and old-time Black country music who helped formulate my ideas must include Kip Lornell, Doug Seroff, Terry Zwigoff, Paul Oliver, Tony Russell, Michael Licht, Dave Freeman, Peter Guralnick, and Samuel Floyd. The staff of the Center for Popular Music, at Middle Tennessee State University, was extremely helpful, especially Ellen Garrison and Sarah Long. Additional thanks must go to Stacey Wolfe for research assistance. Others who helped in various ways and in various parts of the manuscript include: Mrs. Bernice Burns, Mrs. Betty Nokes, Paul Ritscher, W. K. McNeill, W. R. Dunn, Judith Meredith, Joe Webber, Alexandria Penny, Stu Jamieson, Cordell Kemp, Lynn B. Stewart, Bruce Nemerov, Paul Wells, Cindy Wolfe, and Bill Knowlton. Finally, I am pleased to acknowledge the help and support of my wife, Mary Dean Wolfe.

—Charles K. Wolfe

Introductions

I first heard about DeFord Bailey in September 1973. At the time I was employed by the Metropolitan Development and Housing Agency in Nashville. One of my duties was to prepare a newsletter for residents of public housing in the city. A friend, Mrs. Hazel Ferguson, suggested that I include a feature on an elderly Black man named DeFord Bailey, then living in public housing, who, as a young man, "had been a big star" on the "Grand Ole Opry," Nashville's famous radio show. While I had never heard of DeFord Bailey, he sounded like a good profile subject for the newsletter. As I inquired further about him, though, I was given little encouragement. People said he always turned down requests for interviews, that he did no public performing, and that he generally kept to himself. I probably would have dropped the matter at that point, but by chance something happened that stirred my interest even more. I went to Alabama that weekend to visit my parents. I mentioned DeFord Bailey's name to my father, Charles W. Morton; he immediately recognized the name of the legendary Grand Ole Opry star, who he had assumed was long dead. While growing up on a farm in rural Alabama in the 1920s and 1930s, my father had listened to the "Harmonica Wizard" on WSM radio nearly every Saturday night. "I can still remember the sound of DeFord's train," he told me. "It sounded so real that you could almost see it coming down the track."

My father encouraged me to make contact with the Black harmonica player and expressed an eagerness himself to meet DeFord, who in past years brought so much enjoyment to himself and others with his music. With that incentive, I renewed my efforts to meet the retiring performer and to conduct an interview with him.

Mrs. Frances Douglas—the manager of the building where DeFord lived, and a close friend—agreed to try to persuade him to see me. DeFord finally consented, but only after Mrs. Douglas explained that I was "from the Housing Authority" and was writing a "free" newsletter for residents living in housing developments.

Mrs. Douglas then introduced me to DeFord. I immediately liked the small, well-dressed man, and he seemed to like me. I needed only some general information about him to write the brief article for the newsletter, but I spent the entire afternoon with him. Over the next several weeks, I spent many hours with him; we discussed his life, and I eagerly listened to his music when he wanted to play. As I had not yet married, I was able to spend many evenings with him, often staying until midnight or later.

My interest in him led me to research the early history of the Grand Ole Opry. I wanted to verify what DeFord told me and fill in the gaps where his memory was not clear. I went through primary and secondary sources in various Nashville libraries. I also contacted three historians, who provided many facts and materials: Bob Pinson, an archivist with the Country Music Foundation; Dr. Charles K. Wolfe, a country music and blues historian at Middle Tennessee State University; and Dr. Richard Peterson, a sociology professor at Vanderbilt University.

In a number of country music publications, I found DeFord Bailey's role in the history of country music described only in very general terms. The writers emphasized his uniqueness as an early Black country performer, and they referred to his role in the naming of the Grand Ole Opry. Several writers commented on his departure from the Opry, but none adequately explained why he left the show in 1941. They talked about his later career as a shoe-shiner, but said very little about him as an individual, about his background, or about his relationship with other performers.

Most published material about DeFord contained facts taken directly from a short "history" of the Opry written by George D. Hay in the mid-1940s, or from persons who had stopped by DeFord's shoeshine shop in the 1950s or 1960s. These writers had found DeFord unwilling to discuss his earlier career in any detail; some made the erroneous assumption that this reticence was caused by their being white. They thought that DeFord, having been mistreated by the Opry, had come to dislike whites in general.

Confronted with all of this, I felt compelled to try to clear up these misun-derstandings and to see that DeFord Bailey's life and role in country music were adequately and correctly described. My original idea was to collect information, hoping that someone else would use it to publish an article about him. I discussed the matter with Tom Ingram, who at the time was editor of *Nashville!* magazine; he encouraged me to write the article myself, and I did. The result was "Everyday's Been Sunday," published in *Nashville!* in March 1974. In preparing the article, I interviewed a number of DeFord's contemporaries and colleagues on the Opry, many of whom have since passed away; they included Herman Crook, Alcyone Bate Beasley, Roy Acuff, Sam and Kirk McGee, Vito Pellettieri, Sid Harkreader, and WSM executive Jud Collins. The article was well received, and was hailed as the first serious attempt to describe DeFord Bailey's life and career as a whole, to explain the kind of person he was, and to answer some of the questions surrounding his mysterious departure from the Opry in 1941.

"Everyday's Been Sunday" accomplished what I hoped it would. However, because of its brevity, it lacked details about large parts of DeFord's long career. In the following decade, my friendship with the elderly Black musician grew much deeper, and my knowledge much fuller. Throughout this time we talked about the need to write a full-scale biography, and in the months before he died, it became a real concern with him. Almost weekly he asked about my progress on "that book," as he referred to it.

"That book" could be described as DeFord Bailey's "authorized" biography. It was written at his urging, and he reviewed my first draft in some detail. He wanted a biography done so his grandchildren and later generations would know "the truth" about him. The result is basically the story of his life told to me during various visits and conversations. At different times I jotted down notes on scraps of papers, on the backs of envelopes, on whatever was handy when our talks yielded some new fact or detail or quotation that I thought might be included in a biography. Later, I began to more systematically tape record these conversations in his apartment, and eventually I amassed over thirty hours of such recordings. After I moved from Nashville to Dallas, I conducted telephone interviews with DeFord, though many were more conversations than actual interviews; with his permission, I also taped many of these, eventually generating some twenty-five additional hours. These tapes are the sources for most of the direct quotations used in the following pages.

I have detailed, but not dwelt upon, the sadness and misfortune DeFord suffered. "I've come a hard way," he said, when pressed. He himself seldom dwelt on the negative side of things, and neither have I. He preferred to remember the good times he'd had, and his many friends and fans from all over the country. He liked to describe his life in a positive manner: "Everyday's been Sunday."

To convey the full flavor of DeFord's personality and speech, I have used his own words whenever possible. These quotations are clearly the heart of the book. DeFord's vocabulary was limited, and he used the simplest words and phrases in his speech; however, the manner in which he used them conveys tremendous imagery. For example, in describing his speech, he once said, "I never did get upstairs in my talking. I talks just like the Bible. Plain spoken. Nothing to play with or laugh at. Just the plain truth." Like the parables in the Bible, DeFord made frequent reference to the common things around him to illustrate his points. Once in describing how he made a particular note on his harmonica, he compared it to "a shocking spring in a car—it has to go up and down."

DeFord was blessed with a good memory that greatly aided in the preparation of this book. "My momma told me people and animals are kin," he said. "If that's so, then I must be kin to an elephant, because I never forget nothing."

He was, in many ways, a delightful and fascinating personality to write about. He could be light and witty, often laughing at himself, or he could be solemn and serious, sometimes even prophetic about conditions or the times

Through it all, there was an innocence, a childlike quality, that made him a warm and sympathetic figure. He even recognized this in himself. "I never grew up," he explained, "I just got old."

—David C. Morton

I first met DeFord Bailey in the summer of 1973. I was working on my book *Grand Ole Opry: The Early Years* and was trying to talk to as many of the original Opry veterans as I could. Dick Hulan, who was then teaching a summer seminar in folklore at Vanderbilt, took me over to DeFord's high-rise and introduced me. That afternoon DeFord was more interested in playing than talking, and he did a number of tunes on the harp and then got out his banjo and played "Lost John" in an odd, up-picking style I had never seen before. He didn't want to talk much about the early Opry, but he did liven up when I asked him about the kind of music his grandfather played. "Black hillbilly music," he said. "It was all around back then." The phrase stuck with me, and over the years has encouraged me to research this forgotten genre of American music. I look upon this collaboration as yet another chapter in that research.

In later years I went back to visit DeFord several other times, but it was obvious that the person who really had DeFord's confidence was David Morton. I, as well as the entire body of country music historians, was vastly impressed when David's article in *Nashville!* came out. From that point on, David was the reigning expert on DeFord, and we all encouraged him in his continuing research and interviewing. He was doing something no other writer about DeFord had been able to do: getting DeFord to open up and talk candidly about his unique past. The story he uncovered was as rich and fascinating as everyone thought it would be, and three years ago, when David asked me to work with him on it, I was flattered and very willing. It was only after I became involved in the project that I realized just how much time and effort and money David had sunk into his researches. Few biographers have lavished as much time and commitment to a subject as he had, and few have been as close to their subjects.

My job as a collaborator has been to flesh out the historical and cultural context of DeFord's life and music, and to help in structuring the narrative. Along the way, I have delved into my own files about Tennessee ·music, done some new interviews with people who knew DeFord or his times, and prodded David to dig into his notebooks for more quotations and details. We have resisted the temptation to do more than present a straight biography here; a full study of DeFord's complex music, as well as his sociological role as an African American artist in a white-dominated country music culture, will have to wait for future works. We have also tried to gear the book to a general audience, not just one of folk music enthusiasts or ethnomusicologists or Grand Ole Opry fans. DeFord's story, we think, has a universal appeal, and should be seen not as a romantic legend but as a parable of integrity and survival.

—Charles K. Wolfe

1

"The Blues Is a Sad Music"

The procession of cars slowly wound its way down Elm Hill Pike, one of the old meandering Nashville streets that was laid out long before anybody thought of interstate loops or exit ramps. It headed west, moving away from the Cumberland River, away from Music Row with its souvenir shops, music publishers, and big-name record companies. It headed toward a part of Nashville not included in the tour-bus routes or marked on the maps showing the Homes of the Stars. Its destination was the venerable Greenwood Cemetery, Nashville's historic Black cemetery, founded in 1888. One by one, the cars reached the main entrance and began to turn north. It was June 23, 1983.

The cars pulled around to a plot in the front section of the cemetery, and people began to get out and look around. In front of them was a monument draped in white cloth; behind them were the old trees and gentle hills of the back part of the cemetery. To the north, the grounds sloped down to the tracks of the Louisville & Nashville Railroad—appropriate, perhaps, given the love of railroads by the man they had come to honor. Nearby were the graves of Nashville's most illustrious Black leaders: Alexander Looby, the West Indies native who came to Nashville in 1926 and changed forever its civil rights climate; Cornelia Shepherd, one of the leaders of the original Fisk Jubilee Singers, who toured internationally in the nineteenth century helping to promote the appreciation of Black folk music; John Merritt, the amazing football coach at Tennessee State University, who brought the art of coaching to new heights. Then there was the grave of the man who was the center of attention today: DeFord Bailey. Earlier that day, the mayor of Nashville, Richard Fulton, had formally declared the day to be "DeFord Bailey Day," and the metropolitan government had passed a resolution stating what most

DeFord Bailey and Roy Acuff on the Grand Ole Opry. Photograph by Les Leverett.

of the friends gathering in Greenwood already knew: that "Mr. Bailey was the first musician to perform on the Grand Ole Opry," that he "performed for the first recording session ever held in Nashville," and that he "made major contributions to country music and the Nashville community." They also knew that he was one of the most influential harmonica players in blues and country music, that he was one of the most popular figures in the first fifteen years of America's longest-running radio show, "The Grand Ole Opry." They knew, too, that he had paid his dues over the years, traveling and touring under conditions that would appall modern musicians, and that he had endured all this with grace and dignity. And they knew of the one quality that separated him from all the other early country music stars on the Opry: he was Black.

An odd mixture of people began finding their places in front of the podium set by the draped monument. There were members of DeFord's family, his children and grandchildren, and old friends; there were fans, some with cameras and video gear, standing back in respectful silence. There were reporters as well—from the local papers, from the country music trade magazines and journals—and television correspondents like Kenley Jones, from NBC. Then there were the musicians, including many of DeFord's old friends who had toured with him back in

Bailey with harmonica. Photograph by Marilyn K. Morton.

Bailey performing at the Grand Ole Opry. Photograph by Alan Mayor.

the 1930s and listened to his music for years on the Opry. There was Roy Acuff, sharply dressed in a gray sports coat and subdued tie, the official spokesman for the modern Opry, often introduced as "the King of Country Music." There was Bill Monroe, the stately patriarch of bluegrass music, one of the most honored musicians in American culture, dressed in a dark pin-striped suit and without his trademark white hat. There was Herman Crook, leader of the oldest stringband on the Opry, the Crook Brothers Band; there was Kirk McGee, courtly in his well-cut suit and string tie, who had traveled with DeFord and the colorful Uncle Dave Macon in the 1930s; Zeke Clements, the 1930s Opry singer who had gone west

Bailey playing banjo on the balcony of his apartment at I. W. Gernert Homes in Nashville. Photograph by Marilyn K. Morton.

to find a role as the voice of one of the seven dwarfs in Walt Disney's *Snow White.* There were some of DeFord's younger friends, like James Talley, the singer and songwriter best known for his folklike songs about the backroads South, and the author of this book (me), David Morton, a former Vanderbilt history student and housing official, who had been the harmonica player's manager and biographer in the musician's last years. As the musicians began gathering, members of the Crook Brothers Band and Bill Monroe began quietly taking out their instruments, and the Rev. H. L. Parks Jr., DeFord's pastor, greeted family members.

Yet this was no funeral service. DeFord Bailey had died almost twelve months earlier, on July 2, 1982. This was a less solemn memorial gathering, a tribute by friends and family, a dedication, a celebration. This was made clear when I stepped to the podium and said, "Many of you realize that the catalyst for all this was that I promised DeFord some time ago that I would make sure that he had a proper tombstone on his grave." Soon Earl White, the fiddler in the Crook Brothers Band, struck up an old breakdown, "Sugar in the Gourd," and Herman Crook added his own harmonica to the sound. It was a sample of the kind of music that gave birth to the Grand Ole Opry back in 1925, and the

Bailey with Nashville Mayor Richard Fulton following a performance by Bailey for senior citizens living in public housing in Nashville. Photograph given to Bailey by Mayor Fulton.

kind of music that DeFord's grandfather, a champion fiddler, would have liked. After the invocation, Bill Monroe came forward to play a haunting mandolin solo of one of DeFord's most evocative tunes, "Evening Prayer Blues." Monroe told the gathering, "DeFord was the best harmonica player, when it came to playing the blues, of any man, I thought, that ever lived."

Next came the introduction of various special guests. From the Grand Ole Opry were Jerry Strobel and Hal Durham; from the Hohner Harmonica Company, whose instruments DeFord Bailey had always used, was Jack Kavoukian; from Nashville's city hall were Mayor Richard Fulton and

Bill Monroe, Herman Crook and members of his band, Zeke Clements, and Roy Acuff with Bailey monument following its unveiling on June 23, 1983, in Greenwood Cemetery, Nashville. Photograph by Alan Mayor.

Councilman Mansfield Douglas; from Capitol Hill was State Senator Douglas Henry. Uncle Dave Macon's grandson, Ramsey Macon, who had been a pall-bearer at DeFord's funeral, was there. Acuff, coming forward to speak, remembered how he had come to Nashville in 1938 as a young, unknown singer, and how DeFord went with him on the road as "the name act that would draw the audience." He talked about a drive that was currently under way to have DeFord inducted into the Country Music Hall of Fame and assured the crowd

DeFord's immediate family and pastor at dedication of the Bailey monument in 1983. Left to right, Mr. and Mrs. DeFord Bailey Jr., Christine L. Craig, Dezoral Thomas, and the Reverend H. L. Parks Jr. Photograph by Alan Mayor.

that "if his name is ever on the ballot, he'll have one vote from Roy Acuff." The crowd was pleased. They all knew that DeFord had been fired from the Opry in 1941, that he had not played much from then until his death, and that his relationship with the Nashville country music community had not always been cordial. Election to the Hall of Fame, many felt, would be a step toward righting some old wrongs.

James Talley then came forward with his guitar and did an intense version of "John Henry," one of the old songs DeFord liked. From their seats, Herman Crook and Kirk McGee and Zeke Clements patted their feet and remembered times when they too had done the song with that kind of verve and spirit. Then it was time for the mayor, Bill Monroe, and Roy Acuff to step forward and unveil the monument. The design had been donated by artist Rodney Dobbs and the stone prepared by Georgia's Supreme Granite Service, one of the oldest and most respected monument makers. It was a simple but elegant design, a harmonica across a staff of notes, with the legend "HARMONICA WIZARD" on the instrument. "Harmonica Wizard" was the sobriquet given to DeFord back in the 1920s when he first started out on the Opry. Underneath was the text:

Herman Crook and his band performing at the dedication of the Bailey monument in Greenwood Cemetery in Nashville on June 23, 1983. Photograph by Dale Ernsberger: Nashville Public Library, Special Collections.

DEFORD BAILEY
1899–1982
Musician-Composer-Entertainer
Early Star of Grand Ole Opry

People quietly read the inscription, oblivious to the hot sun overhead and the fleecy white clouds racing across the sky. Only the click of Nikon shutters from the photographers broke the silence. Then Herman Crook, the Opry's other veteran harmonica player, himself in his mid-eighties, came up to the microphone and

Roy Acuff with several of Bailey's grandchildren at the dedication of Bailey monument in Greenwood Cemetery on June 23, 1983. Photograph by Alan Mayor.

began blowing his version of "Amazing Grace." It was an appropriate benediction, and people began to reluctantly rise from their chairs. The NBC camera crew headed for the airport, where they had to make a deadline for the network news that evening. The local reporters stayed and asked friends and fans about DeFord and their favorite stories. The Opry old-timers agreed that this was the sort of dignified tribute DeFord would have enjoyed; they thanked me for arranging it. The family, and other friends, prepared to continue to motorcade to the Country Music Hall of Fame, where they would donate to the museum mementos of the entertainer's career: one of the battered metal megaphones that he used to amplify his harp in days before good microphones; three of his hats; a framed business card that had hung in Bailey's downtown shoeshine stand, which he ran after he left the Opry; a walking cane that opened up into a portable chair; and other items. Soon the site was almost deserted, and the cemetery workers, who had postponed work on another funeral for that afternoon, picked up their tools and began to get back to business as usual. Several visitors stayed to talk a bit, reflecting on how the last few true pioneers of Nashville's fabulous country music industry were dying off. Some looked more closely at the handsome printed program I had prepared, with its outline of DeFord's rich career and its reproduction of the harmonica design on the monument. And some read more carefully the inscription on the front of the program, a quotation from DeFord taken from one of the many conversations he had had with me. In it he had tried to speak across the years, to bridge the gap between his world and mine, between a rural Black culture long vanished and a modern world of high-rises and a country music grown into a million-dollar industry. What DeFord had said spoke to all:

> The blues is a sad music. It ain't nothing but you're hard up and can't do nothing for yourself. Like when you're way away from home and try to make it home and can't. Or got children and they're sick and you can't feed 'em and feel bad. Almost a church song. Real serious. Like you're sick and don't know what to do for your family. You go to singing. Calling on the Lord to help. We call it "the blues."

This is how one man coped with that still sad music.

2

"They Didn't Give Me No Rattler, They Gave Me a Harp"

Like many early Grand Ole Opry stars, DeFord Bailey was not born in the Nashville city limits but came from the rough, hilly countryside that loops Nashville like a giant horseshoe. The Bailey family had its roots in Smith County, about forty miles east of downtown Nashville. A beautiful and remote region, it is on the edge of the Cumberland Rim, marked by "knobs" and hollows and crossed by numerous brooks and creeks. The land is filled with cedar groves and rocky fields; its winding roads are lined by old rock fences made of stones the local farmers carried out of their fields. The end of the county where the Baileys lived has as its northern border the Cumberland River, which loops south to form Beasley's Bend near the county seat of Carthage. At the turn of the century, steamboat trade on the Cumberland had made the area a center for logging and wood products, and much of the flat land was given over to tobacco growing; sharecropping was still very much in place as an economic system. About fifteen thousand people lived in the county at this time, and about one thousand of these were Blacks.

Among these were the children of a man named Lewis Bailey, DeFord's paternal grandfather. During the early years of the twentieth century, when DeFord was a young boy, Lewis Bailey lived with DeFord's family and told him stories about the family history. DeFord always felt that one of Lewis's parents was "a full-blooded Indian," probably a Cherokee. "You could tell he [Lewis] was part Indian," DeFord remembered. "He had real straight hair and a high cheekbone." In fact, many of Lewis's children and grandchildren inherited similar features, down to DeFord and to his son, DeFord Jr. "My hair, before it turned gray, was straight and thick. Oh, man! When I was eight years old, they cut my hair off. My plaits was hanging down here [over my shoulders], just as pretty as you wanted to see anything. I had it parted in the middle; it just lay down so pretty and black. I looked like a little Indian boy running around there, hair plopping all over my face and everything."

His grandfather told DeFord that the Bailey name came from a slave owner named Jonathan Bailey in nearby Wilson County, Tennessee. Lewis had been born as a slave near Commerce, a community near Watertown, on the line between Wilson and Smith counties, in 1843. He had been told that his ancestors had been sold into slavery in New York, then dispersed to Alabama, North Carolina, and Tennessee. Lewis was first owned by a man named Butler, then by Bailey; when he was freed in 1863, like many freedmen, he adopted the name of his former owner's family.

Shortly after he was freed, Lewis joined the Union army for the duration of the Civil War. Military and pension records reveal that he, along with many other freed slaves from Middle Tennessee, was signed up for garrison duty in 1864. Most of his time was spent as a teamster at a contraband camp in Gallatin, Tennessee, in neighboring Sumner County; he was mustered out of the service on January 21, 1866. In the meantime, probably before joining the army, he had married a woman named Margaret Newby, a Virginia native and former slave. As Reconstruction began, the couple returned to the area around Commerce, where Lewis had been born, and began their family. Though Lewis was a skilled shoemaker, and was developing into a superb fiddler, he apparently spent most of the next thirty years as a sharecropper or tenant farmer. By the 1890s he was on a farm near the modern community of Brush Creek, just across the county line in Smith County.

Lewis and Margaret would eventually have a total of eighteen children, including two sets of twins. Though some died in infancy, at least half of them reached adulthood and began families of their own. They included Lindy, Lewis, Edward, Margaret, Mandy, Lester, Albert, Barbara Lou, as well as DeFord's father, John Henry Bailey, who was born on May 20, 1878. DeFord didn't know much about his father's early life, but by the time Henry was about twenty, he had met and courted a young woman named Mary Reedy. The Reedy family, headed by Samuel and Sally Reedy, were neighbors of the Baileys near Brush Creek and actually owned the small plot of land they worked. By 1899 Henry and Mary had gotten married and were living near the community of Bellwood; the hamlet itself was just across the county line in Wilson County, astride the old Rome Road, which ran on to the west through the town of Rome and, eventually, to the

Lewis Bailey, DeFord Bailey's grandfather, as he appeared about 1900. From a family photograph belonging to Mrs. Haney Rucks, one of DeFord's first cousins.

Smith County seat of Carthage. The family was actually living in the countryside on the Smith side of the county line, but nearer to Bellwood than anyplace else.

It was there that DeFord was born on December 14, 1899. Family stories told that there was a foot of snow on the ground that day and that a local country doctor, a white man named Dr. Bob Johnson, rode horseback through the snow to reach the small wood-frame farmhouse where the Baileys lived. The birth was apparently without incident (the physical afflictions DeFord suffered would come later), and young Mary Bailey set about choosing a name for her new son. She decided to create a name based on the names of two of her former schoolteachers, a Mr. DeBerry, and a Mrs. Stella Ford. Blending the last names, she came up with DeFord. It was one of the few things she was able to do for her new son. Just over a year after DeFord was born, Mary Reedy Bailey suddenly died of some unknown illness. Shocked and dispirited, Henry Bailey tried his best to care for his young child, but he soon realized that he couldn't do this and earn any kind of a living as a laborer. His family was large and close, though, and soon his youngest sister, Barbara Lou, was helping him out with his baby; over the months, she grew attached to her young nephew, and gradually she took over complete care of the child. She was to do so as long as she lived, and would in effect become his foster mother. Even though she soon married herself, to a local man named Clark Odum, and started her own family, she continued to consider DeFord as "her child." In later years, DeFord knew that the Odums were not his natural parents, but always spoke of them as "my momma and my daddy."

Barbara Lou's love for DeFord was soon put to a test. When the child was three he was stricken with polio. "I couldn't walk for over a year," he recalled. For most of this time he was confined to bed, able to move only his head and his arms. Dr. Johnson, the same physician who delivered DeFord, was called to treat him; Johnson's own son also suffered from polio, and the doctor was skilled in the few techniques available to treat the disease in rural America in 1902. After a time, Dr. Johnson exhausted these remedies and admitted to DeFord's family that there was little more he could do; he didn't want to keep taking their money for such scant results. Barbara Lou didn't give up; like generations of rural mothers before her, she turned to more traditional folk remedies. She tried rubbing DeFord with various homemade lubricants and salves in an attempt to make his body more limber. On one occasion, the family caught an owl, cooked the grease out of it, and rubbed the boy with it; they also tried "polecat grease" and common fishing worms cooked in butter. "They greased me with everything they could think of that was limber," DeFord recalled.

"Some of it must have worked, 'cause I got better." DeFord survived the ordeal and eventually recovered, though the experience seriously stunted his growth—he was always to be smaller than other children his age—and left him with a slightly deformed back. Unlike the doctor's son, though, he did not have to wear braces for the rest of his life.

For the next several years, DeFord led a mellow, bucolic life as he and his foster family moved from farm to farm in the hills of Smith County. As Clark and Barbara Lou Odum started their own family, they lived and worked as tenant farmers or sharecroppers on larger farms owned by white men. One farm was owned by Fuzz Manor, another by Jack Bradford, and another, near Bellwood, by Tom Phillips. Religion came in regular doses from the Methodist Church, and both the Bailey and the Reedy family were large but close-knit, often having informal gatherings. DeFord learned about farm animals and became especially fond of horses. He remembered having, as a small child, two pet German Shepherds who pulled him on his bike like a miniature horse and wagon.

At night he could hear the whistle from the trains on the N.C. & St.L. (Nashville, Chattanooga & St. Louis) line as it crossed the county some four miles to the south, and at other times the baying of the hunting dogs as they chased fox or coon in the nearby hills. Both sounds would later come to haunt him and become a part of his music. So too would the proverbs taught him by his foster parents, proverbs that formed a rural Tennessee version of *Poor Richard's Almanac*. When visiting friends, he was taught, "You should make your visits short and you'll have long friends." About gossip or tale telling, he should remember, "When you say something, be able to say it twice." Other maxims of his foster mother included: "Stay on the ground and you can't fall far"; "A still tongue makes a wise head"; "A good run is better than a bad stand"; "It's better to say there he goes than here he lays." The pragmatic thread running through such proverbs was best illustrated in DeFord's own explication of one of his favorites of these sayings:

You've heard it thunder. You ain't never heard of thunder hurting nobody, have you? You've seen it lightning? That's what can hurt you. What somebody calls you ain't going to hurt you. Don't nothing hurt you but a lick. As long as nobody ain't hittin' on you, just go right on. When they go to hittin' on you, do the best you can for yourself.

In later years, as he forged a career in which he was to challenge social barriers, suffer numerous insults, and hear a lot of "thunder," such advice would become an important part of DeFord's own survival strategy.

Music was also a big part of his Smith County heritage. "Was nothing to do but make music and ride the horses," he later joked. All of his relatives enjoyed music. "They could all sing and dance. Everyone could play at least one instrument." Grandfather Lewis Bailey "was the best fiddle player in Smith County, and was considered a champion fiddler back then." Though he died when DeFord was only eight, his living his last years with the Odums gave the boy ample opportunity to listen to his fiddle tunes and yarns. "He played 'Old Joe Clark,' 'Lost John,' all them way-back pieces, reels, and breakdowns," DeFord recalled. DeFord would soon add these to his own repertoire, as well as other numbers like "Old Hen Cackle," "Fox Chase," "John Henry," and "Comin' 'Round the Mountain." These tunes were not the kind of blues or spirituals stereotypically associated with Black folk music; they were part of a rich tradition of stringband music that was shared by both Blacks and whites in the nineteenth century. In later years, DeFord would call this "Black hillbilly music" and would lament that it was a part of folk music tradition that became virtually extinct with the coming of the blues craze in the 1920s. But in Smith County at the turn of the century, such music was the music of choice for rural Blacks, and DeFord marvelled at the veneration with which his grandfather cared for it. He was even fascinated that his grandfather "would put rattlesnake rattlers loose into his fiddle" to improve the sound—a widely known custom that is still occasionally practiced by southern fiddlers even today.

Though some of his natural mother's folks, the Reedys, played music (his mother could play the guitar, and her brother was considered a good harmonica player), most of DeFord's musical training came down through the Baileys and through his foster family. Lewis Bailey had often entered fiddling contests at local fairs and celebrations, often with one or two of his sons to accompany him. Later, DeFord remembered Clark Odum being "pretty good" on the guitar, banjo, and fiddle; and his foster mother Barbara Lou "sang and played a little, mostly church songs." Two of DeFord's uncles played the harmonica, and one of them, Albert, had the reputation of being the "best harp player in them times." One of his aunts, Mandy, "played the guitar just like a man." For a time several members of the family functioned as a stringband; these included his father, some of his uncles, and one of his aunts. Performing regularly at church gatherings and barn dances, they were favorites at the annual Wilson County Fair in nearby Lebanon.

In fact, DeFord recalled that the Baileys were widely considered to be "the best musicians since slavery times" in that part of the state:

> Whites and Blacks would be playing music and dancing at what you'd call a barn dance—you clean the ground off and put sawdust down on it and make it soft where you can dance. Well, they'd look out and see the Baileys and they'd say, "Here come the Baileys, we'll turn the thing over to them." The whites and Blacks would play some, but they'd put it off to the Baileys to play the most. We was knowed from slavery times as the best musicians.
>
> They would usually have a fiddle, guitar, banjo, harp, mandolin, and drums. They had them great big old drums. Everybody knowed the Baileys could play a harp, a banjo, all string music, piano and bass horns. You know them big old bass horns? Well, my uncle played that. I remember that well myself. A big old brass bass horn.

When the family wasn't playing music in public, they would get together at nights and on weekends. "Many a time we'd just set 'round the fireplace, making music, sometimes cooking sweet potatoes and ash cakes," DeFord recalled. Music would ring late into the night, with different ones singing along, trading off instruments, even doing a type of old-time buck dancing which DeFord remembered later in life. Younger children like DeFord were often put to bed long before the music stopped, "but we never went to sleep 'til it was all over. We would lay in bed listening and keeping time to the music 'til the last tune was played." With his amazing memory and gift for music, DeFord seldom forgot a tune he heard at these gatherings. Even in his old age, he could still recall dozens of tunes he heard on such evenings—old pop songs, blues, religious songs, songs shared by both Black and white traditions, others more associated with Black music. They would help make his later repertoire one of the most diverse and eclectic of the time. "All them things was happiness back then," he would remember.

Ironically, it was through his near-fatal bout with polio that DeFord became a participant in this rich tradition. Even before his illness at age three, he had been "playing around" with instruments. "My folks didn't give me no rattler, they gave me a harp, and I ain't been without one since. Here's how it was. I started as a baby. You know how a baby lays on its back and wiggles its toes? When I'd cry, my mama would give me the harp or the mandolin to play with. She would blow a note on the harp and hand it to me. I played with it like a rattler and liked the sound." After he was stricken with polio, he had to lie in bed for almost a year, nearly disabled. It was then "that I really got started playing music." His father had to find ways to keep him occupied. "My daddy would give me a harp or hang an old guitar or banjo around my neck and let me pick on it for hours at a time. I couldn't do much else. I probably made more noise than music back then, but I've been playing my harp or something ever since then." After his recovery, his frail physical condition led him to keep on with his music. "If I'd been stout, I'd have laid that harp down when I was a boy. Since I wasn't, I stuck with it. At Christmas time, I was always easy to please: I just wanted a new harp."

He soon began to learn how different harps could make subtly different sounds. Though he would come to favor the Hohner Marine Band model (which had been introduced only in 1896, six years before his illness), he soon learned that "harps all look alike, but they're different. You have to fit your mouth different to play every one just like a mold. They blow down different, and come up different." The same harp could even sound different if the weather, even just the humidity, had changed significantly. As a child, DeFord could already detect moisture in his harp—which meant that someone else had been fooling with it. "I could always tell when somebody else played my harp. My foster sisters would play on it some- times. They'd try to put it back just like it was, but I could tell. . . . I learned to blow with a dry breath. I could blow for years and not get no moisture in my harp. My harp never would swell up."

The mouth harp was his favorite instrument, but not his only one. He learned to play the guitar, the mandolin, and even the fiddle a little bit. But in these early days, growing up with his foster brother and sisters in the Cumberland foot- hills, DeFord became adept at using a wide variety of homemade instruments. He recalled:

I had a pretty good banjo one time that was made out of a hoop cheese box and a groundhog skin. My daddy caught the groundhog and dried the skin. Then he stretched it over the hoop cheese box for me. It had a good sound; I'd hold it to the fire and draw it up and make it tight.

Sometimes me and my foster brother and sisters would use mama's wash tubs like bass fiddles. You know, a Number Two wash tub can sound better than a bass fiddle. You drive a hole in the middle of the tub and take you a string and pull it through. Tie a nail to one end of the string to keep it from coming through the tub. Get you a broom handle and tie the other end of the string to it and then pull the string backwards and forwards.

You ever made music with a hair comb? You can put paper over it and blow against it. You holler through it. You can get any tune you want out of it, high or low. I didn't last long with them combs, though, 'cause it tickled my lip.

I bet you never heard of making fiddles out of corn stalks. Well, we did that too.

In the evenings we'd call the cows and goats with cow's and ox's horns.

With some of his homemade instruments, DeFord touched some of the deepest wellsprings of Black folk music traditions. One was the cane fife. "Sometimes we'd make whistles out of canes. You cut 'em off about three inches from one joint to the other, cut a hole in the top and down below, and blow it." Such an instrument, often played to a drum accompaniment, has been found in reports of Black music dating back to the 1820s and might well derive from music of the African coastal nations. Rural fife-and-drum ensembles survived in West Tennessee and northern Mississippi well into modern times. Another very old instrument DeFord remembered was the quills. "If you cut them canes right, you can get what you call a quill and have tunes then, one a little taller than the other. Get one about the size of your finger and cut that one off. Blow it. Then you blow the other one and get your time. Put 'em together and then you go from one to the other, get enough to get a whole song."

Such quills—really a set of short reed pipes closed at one end and fastened together—were also fairly common with rural southern Blacks, but they have fared nearly as well into the modern age. Thomas Talley, the Black Fisk University teacher whose book *Negro Folk Rhymes* (1922) contains an extensive description of quill playing in Middle Tennessee from the turn of the century, refers to them as "probably the Negro's most primitive instrument which he could call his very own." In 1927, the year DeFord would make his first recordings, a Texas musician named Henry Thomas would also record a handful of sides featuring the quills—including a piece called "The Fox and the Hounds" (Vocalion 1137), which bears some fleeting resemblance to DeFord's own "Fox Chase." Many quill players could apparently whoop and hoot as they blew into their quills, and it is possible that young DeFord picked up some of his technique from this practice.

Another venerable instrument was "the bones." "We'd take the two low ribs of a steak, beef ribs. We'd cut 'em so long and dry 'em out in the sun or in the oven, and sandpaper them till they got nice and smooth. Then we'd go out and see who could beat them the best; you can make a pretty good sound clappin 'em between your fingers." Like the fife, the bones can be traced back (in contemporary accounts of Black music) to the dawn of the nineteenth century. They were popular enough to have been incorporated into the instrumentation of commercial minstrel shows by the 1840s. Years later, when DeFord was a star on the Grand Ole Opry, he would run across some polished commercial bones in Chattanooga—one pair made of ivory, one of ebony—and for a time use them in his Opry act. "You know, there's some music in everything," DeFord liked to say. "If we couldn't find nothing else, we could always blow in a jug or beat on some skillets and pans." One of DeFord's cousins was a rural peddler who carried with him an old army bugle that he blew to let people know he was coming. "He would just play a fair tune with that thing," DeFord remembered. "He'd take that bugle and blow it just as pretty as you want to hear anything."

DeFord heard music in everything as well—not only the fiddle music of his grandfather, the harps of his uncle, and guitar of his mother. Even as a boy he tried to duplicate the sounds he heard around the farm. "I caught all that. Sheep. Cow. Chicken. Dog. They got music in 'em. All of 'em. You can get a heavy bass from a cow." He would lie in his bed and hear the sounds of dogs howling, of wild geese honking as they flew overhead, the wind as it blew through the cracks in the wall, the rumble of a distant train. "I'm just like a microphone," he said. "I pick up everything I hear around me." In many ways, the Smith County days formed a rich apprenticeship, and though he was to spend only the first nine years of his life there, DeFord would carry with him many of the tunes and sounds he learned there, and even the imitations he learned would find a place in his later music. He meant it when he summed up his life there by saying, "All them things was happiness back then."

3

"That Boy's Gonna Play That Harp Someday"

In 1908, DeFord's grandfather Lewis Bailey died, and his foster father, Clark Odum, decided it was time to make a move from Smith County. Odum had met George S. Hunt, who had recently bought a farm in Davidson County, around Nashville. "He was a Dutchman," recalled DeFord, "a little short man like me, and he worked for the Marshall-Bruce Company [an office supply company] in Nashville." Impressed with Clark's farming and organizational ability, Hunt hired him to work on his new farm and to be the manager. The farm was located near Newsom's Station, a railroad community on the Harpeth River, about ten miles west of downtown Nashville. "The farm was a big one," DeFord recalled, "about three mile long."

While the Odums prepared to move, DeFord went for a few weeks to stay with his real father, Henry Bailey. Henry had moved to Nashville, where he had remarried; he was living with his second wife, Callie, and their children, Hubie and Maggie, "on First Street across from the ice house" in a section of town called "the Black Bottom." DeFord was not especially impressed with his first stint in the big city, but he was impressed with his means of getting there. Callie Bailey had come out by train to Smith County to get DeFord and bring him back to Nashville. DeFord had heard the train before, on the farm, and realized it was different from the other sounds he heard around the farm; he had even tried to imitate it with his harp. But he had never seen one before and, years later, could remember the experience vividly:

> I didn't see a train 'til I was nine. I had heard the sound before and asked Momma what it was. She said it was a train. When I finally saw a train, I

thought it was the biggest thing I'd ever saw. It got bigger and bigger as it came toward me. It was so big and funny looking that I was half scared of it.

His long ride in from Smith County marked his first real experience with this phenomenon, which would become an important part of his music. Clark Odum was an able and competent farm manager; he ran Hunt's farm near Newsom's Station for six years, from about 1909 to 1915. He hired other Blacks to help out as needed, did a lot of the work himself, and expected his family to weigh in as much as they could. Clark did most of the plowing, with one of three mules, Lisa ("a mean mule that would buck and kick"), Kate, and Julie, or one of the horses, Gray John and Bill. Young DeFord was eager to help out but, because of his size, he had to be careful around the horses. "I learned a lot about farming," he said, "and learned how to grow things if I had to, but I knowed I wasn't cut out for that sort of thing." He was still a small, weakly child; by the time he was twelve he looked as if he were only eight or nine. He was so "small and pitiful" that his family worried about his future. "I don't know what's gonna come of you," Barbara Lou told him. "You can't work like your daddy."

However, DeFord did what he could around the farm. He helped out with housework, fed the chickens, milked the cows; occasionally he helped out in the fields, chopping weeds or pulling corn, but seldom doing any "hard work" like plowing with mules. He learned how to cook at a very early age, a skill that would serve him well in later life, and soon was helping out with this. He was also skilled with his hands. When his foster mother worried about his prospects, he used to reassure her: "I told her that I could take things that white people throw away, fix 'em up, and sell 'em back to them. Somehow, I knowed I could take care of myself." He also continued to play his harmonica. By now he was spending several hours each day practicing.

I don't see how my momma and daddy put up with me playing things over and over, and trying different notes, but they did. Sometimes my daddy would ask my momma, "Don't you ever get tired of him playing?" But she'd say, "Mind your own business. He's mine." Other times, she would hide my harp from me, thinking I was harming myself by playing it so much, but I'd just fish around and find it. Then my daddy would laugh and tell my momma, "That boy's gonna play that harp someday!"

Bailey as a youth. Photograph given to Morton by Bailey for use in biography.

When he was "ten or eleven years old," DeFord first played his harmonica for somebody other than family or close friends. He played for "two white boys" who had heard about him and came to hear him play. Impressed, they spread the word, and before long everybody in that part of the country knew about him; "people come from twenty miles 'round to hear me," he remembered. Many of his fans were would-be harmonica players themselves, and after they listened to DeFord, some of them ended up giving him their harps when they left. "You can do more with them than we ever could," they told him. At first, DeFord was puzzled by such tribute; he didn't understand why everyone couldn't do what he could do with a harp. He even tried to learn from other players. "I tried to learn more about my harp from other people when I was a boy, but I didn't learn very much. I thought they didn't want to help me. Later on, I realized that most of them couldn't help me. I was in a different class." During this time, the harmonica was really coming into its own as a popular instrument. "A lot of folks played the harp back then," DeFord remembered. "You could get the best kind of harp for a quarter back then, and nearly everybody had one."

In fact, the years of DeFord's youth coincided with what many historians feel was the high-water mark of harmonica popularity in the United States. The basic instrument that DeFord and most of his friends referred to by the term "harp" was essentially a ten-hole "free reed" instrument that could produce most of the notes of the scale by a combination of exhaling and inhaling. In the most basic or "diatonic" harmonica, a performer can range over three octaves on the scale, but cannot reach all the notes, nor all the sharps or flats. In both the low and high octave, the scale is "gapped" through the omission of certain notes, but a skillful player can "bend" certain notes through overblowing and lip manipulation to pick up accidentals and gapped notes. In the 1920s, after DeFord had already evolved his style, the so-called "chromatic" harmonica was devised; this allowed a player, through the use of a lever device, to pick up all the sharps and flats on a scale. This new type of instrument was the sort featured by various pop music harmonica stars, such as Lou Adler, Johnny Puelo, and jazzman Toots Thielemans. In his later career, DeFord experimented with chromatic harps but rejected them as needlessly complicated. "I didn't need them," he said. "I could do everything they could do on my regular harp."

Forerunners of the modern harmonica have been traced back to Asia over a thousand years ago, but the "mouth organ" as we know it today dates from early nineteenth-century Europe. In 1821, Berlin musician and inventor Christian Friedrich Buschmann made an experimental instrument with fifteen reeds that he called an *Aura,* designed mainly for use as a tuning instrument or pitch pipe. It attracted the attention of a local clockmaker, Christian Messner; due to a depression in the clock-making industry, Messner was looking for other ways to make a little money and began making copies of Buschmann's Aura to peddle at county fairs and inns. This proved lucrative, and soon other grassroots entrepreneurs across Germany were getting in on the act. At first all the instruments were handmade, with the wooden body carved by hand and the reeds painstakingly beaten from brass wire. In 1857, Matthias Hohner (1833–1902) entered the field and figured out a way to use mass-production techniques to make the instruments; his business mushroomed, and soon he was establishing himself as the leader in the field. Within twenty years, he was producing over 700,000 harmonicas a year, and of these over 60 percent were being exported to America. Years later, one of his most satisfied customers would be young DeFord Bailey.

Americans had taken the harmonica to heart from the very first; an instruction manual had been published in New York as early as 1830. By the 1880s this fascination had reached epidemic proportions. An 1890 mail-order musical-instrument catalog issued by the J. R. Holcomb Company of Cleveland devoted two entire pages to harmonicas and their accessories. "The 'mouth-organ' is now recognized as an instrument capable of some of the most refined musical effects," read the copy, "and is becoming more popular every day in all classes of society."

The catalog offered the cheapest instrument for $3.00 "per Doz. by express" and offered to send seven different sample harmonicas for $2.00 postpaid; the most expensive instrument listed, the "Artists Professional Concert" model, cost 70 cents each, or $5.90 per dozen. Also listed were "sounders," or soundboards for the instruments, and "yokes" used to hold the harmonica around the neck while the performer played the guitar or piano. By the turn of the century, other general mail-order houses such as Sears and Montgomery Ward were offering harmonicas at similar prices, and throughout rural America, peddlers and general stores could not keep the little instruments in stock.

There were a number of reasons for the instrument's popularity. Harmonicas were small and eminently portable, a concern in a society where many settlers were still following the frontier. They were available in different keys, which allowed them to be played in combination with other instruments, as with different singing styles. They were relatively durable, able to endure bending or even boiling and still produce music. In the South, the harmonica could be used as a substitute for a fiddle in a stringband while having none of the adverse moral or religious connotations of the fiddle, which many rural preachers had dubbed "the devil's box." The harmonica was especially popular in Middle Tennessee, where churches had an unusually strong aversion to the fiddle.

In eastern Kentucky and southwest Virginia, by contrast, it was not all that unusual for a local fiddler to bring his instrument into church and play during services or for "specials"; this seldom happened in Middle Tennessee. The harmonica, on the other hand, was fully acceptable in church music in Middle Tennessee; in fact, a church near Carthage, not far from where DeFord grew up, boasted a "harmonica quartet" in which four players performed the four-part harmony from gospel songbooks.

The harmonica was also especially popular among rural Blacks, making it what musicologist Harold Courlander called in his *Negro Folk Music USA* "probably the most ubiquitous of Negro folk instruments." According to harmonica historian Michael S. Licht, the instrument was well established in African American folk music as early as the 1870s, and soon after that, Black players began to develop unorthodox playing techniques that included overblowing and playing in what older musicians called "choked" style. In the latter technique, the harp is played a fourth below its intended pitch and is brought closer to a "blues tonality" by manipulating the air stream with the lips or tongue. Imitations also became a staple of early harmonica players; W. C. Handy, the blues composer, remembers growing up in northwestern Alabama in the late 1870s and hearing "French harp" players do imitations of trains and fox hunts. In fact, blues historian Paul Oliver has suggested that the popularity of the harmonica with Black folk musicians might have led to its replacement of the fiddle in rural Black music. Once the dominant instrument among Black folk musicians before the Civil War, the fiddle gradually fell from favor toward the end of the century, just as the harmonica became popular. As we will see, many of DeFord Bailey's harmonica tunes were adapted from his grandfather's fiddle tunes—a process that might not have been at all atypical.

After spending some six years at Newsom's Station, DeFord's family moved again. George Hunt had bought another farm, about twenty-five miles southeast, near the town of Franklin, and he had been so pleased with Clark Odum's work that he persuaded him to bring his family and come down to the new place. Thus, about 1914, DeFord found himself moving to Williamson County, on a major road called Carter's Creek Pike, which is today State Highway 246. The countryside was quite different from Smith County; located in the so-called Nashville Basin, it was a county of broad, rolling fields, known for its walking horses and its history. A major Civil War battle had been fought near Franklin, and the town had preserved much of its nineteenth-century beauty and historic architecture. Williamson County was much more thickly populated than Smith County, and it contained a much higher percentage of Blacks; Smith County, in the 1920 census, had a less than 12 percent Black population; Williamson County in 1920 had a Black population of between 25 and 30 percent. The area also seemed to be a hotbed of Black folk music. Grand Ole Opry stars Sam and Kirk McGee grew up a few miles from Carter's Creek Pike. They would later perform often with DeFord—and they learned much of their instrumental techniques from Black guitarists and fiddlers in the area. As late as 1975, Kirk McGee was able to identify at least twelve Black fiddlers still living in the Franklin area.

DeFord thus began to meet musicians other than those in his family. One of them, the one who "was in the same class" musically as himself, was a crippled boy, Ben Lee Hughes, nicknamed "Tip." DeFord and other friends would pull Tip around town in a little wagon, playing their harmonicas for anyone who wanted to hear them. "We was real close," said DeFord. "He was as good as I was. Sometimes we'd ride all around on the wagon—we'd have two chairs on the platform—and we'd play duets on our harps for people. They would really love that; they gave us lots of tips!" Tip played in a style similar to that of DeFord but never did develop the kind of sharp, dextrous clarity that marked the Bailey sound. DeFord rather liked these first tentative inroads into public entertaining, but Tip was not as enthusiastic. "He was a good harp player, but didn't try to spring out like I did. [Later] I tried to get him to come blow with me on the Opry, but he wouldn't come. He run a grocery store in Franklin and stayed there; I used to send him harps."

Such informal street-corner playing was common during the early 1920s, when folk musicians were just beginning to find ways to make money with their music; many referred to it as "busking," and though few could match the colorful image of two small Black harmonica players holding forth from a wagon platform, the idea itself was hardly new. In centers like New Orleans and Memphis, jazz and blues bands were often hired to travel around the downtown streets in wagons, playing their music to attract a crowd for a dance or a political speech. DeFord's work with Tip Hughes lasted only about a year, but it set him to thinking about whether he could ever make a real living as a "musician."

DeFord's growing fascination with his harp interfered with his schooling. "My schooling was just like going in the front door and coming out the back," he said. "I liked to play my harp in school; the teacher got on me at first, but she finally gave up. I didn't study nothing else but my harp." He attended rural schools in Smith County, at Newsom's Station, and then on Carter's Creek Pike; this was, however, during an era when the average rural school term in Tennessee for whites was only 110 days a year, and for Blacks less than 65 days a year—only about three months. Nor did DeFord have much interest in the basic subjects: "They tried to teach me reading, writing, and arithmetic, but I was only interested in the arithmetic. . . . I wanted to learn how to keep people from beating me out of my money. But they beat me anyhow. I did learn enough arithmetic to count my money and enough reading and writing to sign my name, but that was about it."

Most of what he did learn in school took place during the time he was living on Carter's Creek Pike. He went to the nearby Southall School "for a while," and then to the Franklin Training School. Here he found the only class he really enjoyed: a "manual training" class taught by a Mr. J. K. Hughes. As a child, DeFord had been fond of making things with his hands. "I could drive nails when I wasn't much more than a baby," he said, recalling that he made many of his own childhood toys. Now he was delighted to find that he could actually hone his woodworking skills in a formal class. One of the first things he made was a set of children's furniture consisting of a bed, a dresser, a chest of drawers, and a folding ironing board. He was pleased with his work, as was his teacher, and later DeFord was able to sell the set for the then-impressive sum of $2.75.

Even though he lacked many tools (his mainstays were a hammer and a hand-saw), he continued to work away at building furniture, even at home at night; often he used wood from apple crates or cigar boxes that people had thrown away, again proving the boast he had made to his mother that he could always survive by taking "things that white people throw away, fix 'em up, and sell 'em back to them." He also developed the ability to work with willow: "I had a picture in my mind of what I wanted to make and I'd just do it. I made some willow tables and chairs that way that was real fancy, too; you know, you can bend willow any way you want to." Each year, Mr. Hughes's class would have an exhibition, with a prize given for the best furniture. Both of the years that DeFord attended class, he won the prize, $2.50; one year his prize-winner was a dresser made from discarded apple crates.

After a couple of years on Carter's Creek Pike, DeFord's family moved to another farm, "the Ross Alexander place," a few miles east near the community of Thompson's Station. The town was seven miles due south of Franklin, on the L&N Railway line between Nashville and Birmingham. By now DeFord was a teenager—even though he was only four-and-a-half feet tall and weighed less than ninety pounds—and was starting to look around for some kind of steady employment.

Like many rural children, he had to walk a long distance to school every day, and one day, when he was walking along with twenty-five or thirty other children, he was stopped by a white store-owner named Gus Watson. "I was always behind; I stayed out of the crowd. He [Watson] would see us going to school. He called me from the porch one day and when I come to him, he asked me if I wanted to be a houseboy. I told him I did. I went home and asked my daddy, and he said that it'd be fine." Shortly thereafter, DeFord moved in with Mr. Watson and his wife, Cora; soon he was spending nearly all his time there, and before long the three had become very closely attached to each other.

> I didn't get a salary, but I got whatever I wanted. He handled me like I was his child. He'd give me a little money now and then, and I'd get whatever I wanted from the store.
>
> I lived in the house with them. I had a cot in the dining room and would sleep there. She'd comb my hair and dress me up to go to school. I went with

them to visit their relatives and friends. I was like their child. I stayed with 'em except when I'd go home sometimes on Sunday evening.

DeFord also helped out some in Watson's general store, doing odd jobs and playing his harp for Watson or his customers. Watson had not known about his houseboy's abilities on the harmonica when he hired him, but he soon learned and was delighted to have a musician around. As it turned out, Watson carried a line of harmonicas in the store and invited DeFord to have as many as he wanted, free of charge. For the first time in his life, DeFord had more harmonicas than he "knowed what to do with." His favorite continued to be Hohner's Marine Band, which Watson sold for twenty-five cents. "It was the best in the world," DeFord remembered. "I've had all kind of harps; I've had them roller harps and all, but ain't nothing beat this harp. It had a good ring to it."

DeFord stayed with the Watsons for about a year—one of the happiest times of his childhood. Then, in 1918, a series of major shocks hit the young musician. On July 30, word came that his natural father, Henry Bailey, had died; Henry had left Nashville and moved to Evansville, Indiana, where he had worked as a laborer. Though DeFord hardly knew his real father, he helped with the funeral arrangements and felt the loss; Henry was brought back from Evansville to be buried, as the death certificate said, in the "Bailey Cemetery" in Smith County. Then Clark Odum decided to make a major change in his life by taking a job in Nashville and moving his family with him. DeFord was expected to join them, which meant an end to his stay with the Watsons, but a third event intervened. In September, just before the war in Europe ended, an epidemic of influenza broke out; it apparently originated in Europe, moved into the eastern United States, and swept through forty-six states, causing panic and eventually claiming some 500,000 lives. It was especially virulent in the South, particularly in parts of Tennessee. Gus and Cora Watson were two who contracted it; they were sick for several weeks and almost died. DeFord managed somehow not to contract the flu and spent all of his time nursing the Watsons: he cooked for them, washed and ironed their clothes, waited on them, and prepared their medicines. During this time, DeFord's own family had to go ahead and move to Nashville, but, seeing that the Watsons were totally dependent on him, DeFord chose to stay behind and help out until the Watsons were well.

In time the Watsons did recover, and they were forever grateful to DeFord for his help. They hated to see him leave Thompson's Station but told him that he and his family would always be welcome to return if things didn't work out in

Nashville. "They promised to give me a field of land near them to live on if I ever wanted to return," DeFord recalled. "They even put me in their will." But DeFord was curious about the "big city" of Nashville and eager to try his luck there, so finally he left to join his family in their new home. Though he was never to move back to Thompson's Station, he kept in touch with the Watsons as long as they lived and always stopped by to see them when he passed through town.

4

"I Wasn't Cut Out
for Most Jobs"

When DeFord arrived at Nashville's Union Station in the late fall of 1918, he was not quite nineteen years old. As he rode in on the train, he noticed that his feet could still not reach the floor when he sat on the seat. Ticket agents insisted on charging him half fare—a child's fare—even though he protested. "I would tell 'em I was grown, but they didn't believe me. I was so little!" In spite of this, he was eager to rejoin his foster family and to see what kind of new job Clark Odum had landed.

The Nashville he traveled through that fall was a bustling little city, a combination of New South and Old South, of modernism and tradition. Its downtown was dominated by the imposing state capitol, built in the 1850s on a hill overlooking the Cumberland River basin; just behind the capitol, however, was the Gay Street area, the town's red-light district and one of its more violent slums. Streetcar tracks and Model T Fords clogged the narrow brick streets, yet at the foot of Broadway, steamboat packets still unloaded goods at docks on the Cumberland just as they had for a hundred years, and in the south end of town the National Foxhunters Association still held field trials for their hounds. Though it had its share of fine theaters and auditoriums, such as the stately Ryman Tabernacle on Fifth Avenue, where the great opera singers were always booked, Nashville was not especially known for its music. Boosters called it the "Athens of the South" and bragged about its colleges and cultural institutions; much of its "old money" came from insurance, banking, and printing. In East Nashville, increasing numbers of young families from the countryside were settling in, taking jobs at the local factories. In four strictly defined enclaves lived the Black portion of Nashville's population—about 30 percent of the total population in 1920; lifestyles ranged from the squalor of the "Black Bottom" near the river to the sedate academia of the Fisk University neighborhood. In large mansions far out on West End Avenue and in the southern suburbs lived the well-to-do businessmen and politicians whose families made up the society pages of the Nashville newspapers, and it was to one of these neighborhoods that DeFord found himself going on that cold fall day. Though he didn't know it at the time, he was to establish a residency that was to last the rest of his life.

Clark Odum had parlayed his horticultural experience into a job with one of Nashville's more prominent families, Mr. and Mrs. J. C. Bradford. The Bradfords were well known in financial circles, and Bradford's company would eventually take over Nashville's first skyscraper, on Church Street downtown, and lend their name to it. They lived in a twenty-room mansion just south of Nashville on Franklin Pike and had hired Clark Odum to care for their yard, grounds, and garden. As was customary at the time, he and his family were furnished a house "on the place" so he could be near his work. Clark had arranged for DeFord to be a "houseboy" for the Bradfords, and DeFord soon found himself in a setting that must have seemed dreamlike to a boy who had hardly ever been out of the country. As he recalled years later:

> They was rich people. Mrs. Bradford had a Packard automobile, a straight eight. That was the best they had back then. You could hardly tell it was moving. It had glass betweeen her and the chauffeur. When she traded cars, the chauffeur would drive her to Detroit to get a new car and then bring it back.
>
> The Bradfords' house was really something, too. It was a mansion and had so many fine things. It had an intercom system with bells in every room to let the help know when they was wanted. They had real fancy furniture, too, the finest; even had two big organs, and they had a bunch of folks working in the house taking care of everything.

At first, his work as a houseboy involved things like running errands, helping to set tables, cleaning and polishing silver, washing and waxing the car, and occasionally opening the door to greet guests. He never actually wore a uniform, but he soon took his place among the Bradfords' large staff of Black "help." Then Mrs. Bradford learned what he could do with a harmonica.

One day I was in the yard and she heard me playing. She said, "I didn't know you could play like that. How long have you been playing?" I told her, "All my life." From then on, she had me stand in the corner of the room and play my harp for her company. Before she found out I could play, I had to work like the rest of the help. From then on, I just fooled around. I'd wear a white coat, black leather tie, and white hat. I'd have a good shoeshine. That all suited me. That's my make-up. I never did no more good work. My work was playing the harp.

As the Bradfords entertained the cream of West End society, DeFord would quietly stand in the corner of the dining room and play—not the blues or rowdy numbers like "The Fox Chase" but nostalgic parlor songs like "Swanee River," "Sweet Marie," and "Sweet Bye and Bye."

DeFord was also fascinated with the two organs in the house and before long was figuring out how to play them. "I'd make 'em just ring," he said. "I'd play religion songs like 'Swing Low, Sweet Chariot.' I'd work my feet and pull them things up there." It was the first organ DeFord had ever seen. "There wasn't none of them in Black churches back then." Some of the girls who worked on the staff showed him how to play the instruments, and soon, DeFord recalled, "I was about as good on it as I was on my harp."

Possibly because of these experiments, DeFord, urged on by an old childhood buddy named Luther Mayberry, decided to try taking piano lessons. It was to be his only brush with formal musical training, and it was a disaster: "That woman ain't taught me nothing. She come out with them *do re me's* and I didn't know one from another. 'Doggone them *do re me's,'* I said to myself. I tried and tried. I couldn't carry a tune in a bucket like she taught. I couldn't handle that stuff."

By this time Clark Odum had taken another job and moved his family from the grounds of the Bradford mansion. Nearby, however, on the same Franklin Road was the house of another wealthy citizen, W. W. Berry, owner of a downtown drug company and chairman of the board of directors of the American National Bank. DeFord's friend Luther Mayberry was working there as a houseboy, and when the Odums moved, Luther suggested DeFord apply for a job at the Berrys' home. He got the job and later recalled that the Berry place was possibly even more impressive than the Bradfords'.

In 1923, however, Barbara Lou Odum died. The Odum family, just beginning to really establish themselves in Nashville, was devastated, but for DeFord the loss was especially keen. Not only was Barbara Lou his favorite aunt, she was his foster mother, the only real mother he had ever known—the person who had single-handedly brought him through his bout with polio and who had defended his incessant harmonica practicing before the rest of the family. Years later he would recall her strong, positive influence on his life, summing up her and Clark Odum as "good honest, hardworking Black people" who were "well thought of by Blacks and whites alike." But with her death, the Odum family began to drift apart. Clark decided to try his luck in Detroit, where thousands of other southerners, white and Black, were going to work in Henry Ford's automobile factories. Before he left, he rented a house in Nashville for DeFord and his other children, most of whom were then in their late teens or early twenties (DeFord was twenty-four). There were a few weeks of uncertainty, but soon word came that Clark had indeed obtained a job in Detroit, and before long he was mailing back to the family a portion of his wages each payday.

Between 1920 and 1925, DeFord found himself working at a variety of jobs in downtown Nashville. For a few months he worked at the old King Pharmacy at Douglas Corner, doing odd jobs and running errands; one of his friends there was a young white boy, Orville Nugent, who worked as the soda jerk. Years later, Nugent recalled: "I was in high school at Hume-Fogg, and lived out in Waverly and I was working in the afternoons at King's. . . . I would open up there in the morning and wait for Dr. King to get there. DeFord would usually be waiting for me to open up and go in to build a fire and clean up. I'd let him in and we'd stand there and talk till the doctor would get there." Several years later Nugent would go to work as an accountant for the National Life & Accident Insurance Company and would help out in the evenings by answering phones and taking telegrams when the company's new radio station, WSM, opened. He would be amused to note that his work would help validate his old friend as one of the station's new stars.

For a time, DeFord returned to his houseboy work, signing on with a family named Jones on Benton Avenue, two blocks from King's; off and on for several years he worked for them—cooking, running errands, and doing light yard work. Then there was a stint working in the kitchen at the venerable Maxwell House Hotel, the 1869 showcase still considered in the 1920s to be the city's most elegant. For several months he worked at the Starr Theater, a motion-picture house on Cedar Street, sweeping up, taking tickets, and even selling popcorn; his cousin, Hurley Seay, helped run the theater. Later he shined shoes in Simmon's Barber Shop on Third Avenue North, made deliveries for a dental supply company on Eighth, and washed cars for a place called Auto Laundry. Whatever job he worked at, he always had his harmonica handy.

I never had a job in my life that I couldn't play around on. I had to play my harp some. It didn't matter what I was doing, I always carried my harp with me. My daddy always told me, "When you work, work; and when you play, play." I didn't play while I was working, but whenever we stopped to eat or take a break, I'd pull out my harp and start blowing on it. One time I was working for a white feller in a cornfield and he told me that if I worked for him, I'd have to leave my harp at home. Well, I told him, if I do, I'll have to stay at home with it. I meant it, too.

In his free time, he discovered Nashville's theaters and other attractions, and he found himself listening to new types of music he had never heard in Smith County. He was especially attracted to the medicine shows that customarily set up in a big tent on South Street in the Edgehill district. Such medicine shows were venues for both white and Black musicians attempting to professionalize their music; throughout Tennessee, these shows were important channels for music styles and songs; in West Tennessee, bluesmen like Gus Cannon worked them, while in East Tennessee, they were training grounds for early country singers like Jimmie Rodgers and Tom Ashley. The organizers of the shows offered free music and comedy as a draw for crowds to which they could sell their self-styled "medicine"—tonics ranging from genuine herbal cures to thinly disguised moonshine. DeFord remembered: "They called them Quaker Doctor shows, and you heard some of the finest singing and dancing there." He learned far more from the free medicine shows than he did from his formal piano lessons.

Another favorite spot was the Bijou Theater in downtown Nashville. This was the main Black theater in town; here DeFord first heard some of the great early singers and musicians from the newly developing area of Black popular music, which in the 1920s was primarily jazz and blues. The theater was owned by a white Nashvillian, Milton Starr, who was to play an important role in the development of the blues. In 1921, Starr had joined forces with Charles Turpin, best known as a St. Louis ragtime pianist and composer, to take over and manage a string of Black theaters in the South and Midwest that made up a circuit called Theater Owners' Booking Agency, or T.O.B.A. By the turn of the century, many of the big vaudeville chains like Keith-Orpheum were beginning to realize that there was a huge new potential audience among the increasing number of Blacks settling in southern cities, and were occasionally booking acts to appeal to them. Their theaters, though, were still strictly segregated, with Black customers having to watch from "peanut galleries" and the like. There was a real need for a Black theater system, and in 1909 two Memphis promoters, the Barrasso brothers, organized the original T.O.B.A.

The system flourished, and the agency was soon providing regular employment for Black repertoire companies, jazz bands, jugglers, tumblers, snake charmers, comedians, and dancing troupes of chorus girls. Pay was low, working conditions deplorable, and soon musicians were joking that T.O.B.A. really meant "Tough On Black Asses." But among the artists showcased on the circuit were the first generation of great blues singers. The "Midnight Ramble," a late show spotlighting blues singers, became a regular feature at many T.O.B.A. theaters, as did special Thursday-night shows set aside for white audiences only. After Starr and Turpin took over, many of the theaters sponsored blues-singing talent contests, giving local musicians a crack at the big time. "Toby time," as singers liked to call it, was an essential conduit for Black music in the 1920s. Blues historian Paul Oliver has noted that "almost all the classic blues singers worked the 'Toby time' . . . at some stage in their careers, and its rigorous schedule of one-week stands gave them a hard but professional testing ground."

DeFord haunted the Bijou and, in fact, even worked there on occasion. Fascinated with the singers, Bailey picked up more than a few songs from them. To advertise the shows, Starr would have posters and window cards made up, many printed at the legendary Hatch Show Print in downtown Nashville. Hatch's files still exist for many of the shows DeFord saw; they offer a detailed account of the singers the young harmonica player might have seen in the early 1920s. In 1924, for example, book-ings included the Chicago blues singer and Paramount recording artist Edmonia Henderson, whose "Black Man Blues" was added to DeFord's repertoire; Hooten & Hooten, comedians whose "Brother Low Down" sermons were all the rage, and who recorded for Columbia; Clara Smith, "the world's champion moaner," the Columbia artist who was one of a number of blues singers named Smith, none related to each other; "Broadway Rastus," actually a white ragtime pianist named Frank Melrose who recorded for Paramount in 1923; Ma Rainey, the veteran blues singer who had been singing blues since 1902 and whose vaudeville performances and many recordings made her the first of the great classic blues singers; and Sammie Lewis, another record artist, with his Creole Steppers jazz band. In 1925, Bijou bookings included the most famous blues singer of all, Bessie Smith; Chicago blues yodeler Charles Anderson; the jazzy patter singing of Butterbeans & Susie, well-known record makers; and singers Sara Martin, Mamie Smith, and Virginia Liston, all of whom recorded for major record labels.

Bailey as a young radio star. Photograph given to Morton by Bailey for use in biography.

Milton Starr was always looking for new talent, and while DeFord was working for him in 1923, he had a chance to hear DeFord play the harmonica. Starr was more than casually impressed and soon came to Bailey with an offer: he wanted him to join the "Toby time" tour and work the circuit as a full-time professional. Still struggling with a series of menial jobs, DeFord was tempted. It was a chance to do exactly what he had decided he wanted to do, be a full-time musician, and it was a chance to actually work with some of the impressive Black stars he had admired. He talked it over with his cousin, Hurley Seay, the only person he knew well who knew anything about the theater business. Seay also talked to Starr about it. Later he pointed out to DeFord that the T.O.B.A. often did live up to its nickname, and that the touring life would be hard, especially for a young, inexperienced twenty-three-year-old harmonica player who was barely four-feet-ten and weighed less than one hundred pounds. He finally advised DeFord not to go off on the tour unless he had a partner; DeFord didn't, and so he reluctantly turned down Starr's offer. Years later, DeFord would wonder how his career might have been different had he made the tour and moved into the mainstream of commercial blues and jazz. But an accident of fortune had placed him in a town where the blues was to take a back seat to another indigenous musical form that was struggling to define itself: country music. Already under way were events that would lead him to find a place in it.

In 1924 and 1925, DeFord found himself working as an elevator operator at the old Hitchcock Building in downtown Nashville. As usual, he found time to play his harp, and soon everybody who rode the elevator was being entertained by his remarkable music. In fact, it was said that certain people who worked downtown found excuses to visit the Hitchcock Building just to hear the elevator man's music. One of the regular riders was a "Miss Maggie"—probably Margaret Welch, the secretary to Charles R. Clements, who had recently been made vice-president and comptroller of the National Life & Accident Insurance Company. National Life was one of the leading insurance companies in Nashville—indeed, in the South—and though it had over one hundred branch offices around the country, it was headquartered in Nashville, in a brand-new five-story building dedicated in February 1924. In the spring of 1925, the company was having a formal dinner at the new building; Miss Maggie invited DeFord to play at it. He agreed and was paid $5 for his work. He thought little enough of it at the time and returned to work as usual the next day; years later, though, he was to look back on the event as an odd foreshadowing of things to come.

5

"The World's Pet"

Radio came to Nashville in the fall of 1925. It was a new, sensational industry that had been spreading like wildfire across the nation since 1920, and people everywhere were talking about "the miracle of radio." Since 1922 major southern cities like Dallas, Atlanta, and Memphis had boasted of broadcasting stations, and in the uncluttered air of the mid-1920s, their signals could easily be picked up by listeners in Nashville. For a city that prided itself on its colleges and cultural institutions and called itself "the Athens of the South," having to settle for radio programs from rival cities was hardly a boost to civic pride. It was heartening, then, for Nashvillians to read in their evening papers in late summer that plans were underway to open not one but two broadcasting stations. The more ballyhooed one was to be started by the National Life & Accident Insurance Company; it was the brainchild of young Edwin Craig, recent Vanderbilt graduate and son of the company president, Cornelius Craig; Edwin, recently made head of the company's life insurance division, had become fascinated with radio, and urged the company to open its own radio station. In the earliest days of commercial radio, stations were often owned outright by companies like Sears in Chicago (WLS) or the *Atlanta Journal* (WSB) in Atlanta. The older veterans at National Life saw little to the idea but finally gave in to placate Craig and to let him have what one of them called "his toy." Work was soon started on the station itself, on the fifth floor of the new building where Bailey had played just weeks earlier.

In the meantime, though, a store in downtown Nashville got the jump on National Life by starting its own station. L. N. Smith had started a radio supply store at 164 Eighth Avenue North called "Dad's"; the newspaper ads of the time featured a character called "Radio Dad" and emphasized that the shop sold any and all parts needed for building your own radio—still the most common way for people in mid-1925 to get decent receiving sets. The manager of the store was Fred "Pop" Exum, a natural entrepreneur and early supporter of radio as a mass medium. He had convinced Smith to get into the radio supply business to start with—earlier he had run an auto supply store—and now urged Smith to start a radio station. If Nashvillians could hear their friends and neighbors on a radio station, it would naturally increase sales and promote radio listening in general. Smith finally agreed that the idea sounded good, and he and Exum set up a small station with the call letters WDAD— featuring the name "DAD"—as well as the store slogan "We Double a Dollar."

WDAD's transmitting equipment came from station WOAN in Lawrenceburg, Tennessee. This station, one of the first in the state, was the vehicle of gospel songbook publishing giant James D. Vaughan and was located about seventy miles south of Nashville, near the Alabama state line. Exum had learned that it was upgrading its equipment and talked Smith into buying the old equipment; Smith and Exum actually drove down to Lawrenceburg and carried it back on a Saturday. A WOAN engineer later came up and helped the men reassemble the equipment on the second floor of the radio supply shop. On September 13, the new station took to the air, opening a new chapter in Nashville music. Though WDAD had only 150 watts of power, at night it could be heard for hundreds of miles, and within days the station was receiving mail from New York, Philadelphia, Des Moines, Atlanta, and Dayton.

Pop Exum was one of DeFord's fans; he had met him when DeFord had come into the auto accessories shop on various occasions to buy parts for his bicycle (his main mode of transportation around town). DeFord always had his harmonica with him and often played a tune or two; Exum had noted how popular he was with customers, and once the new station was going, he wasted no time in asking DeFord to perform on the air. DeFord readily agreed and soon made his debut on WDAD; it was "no time at all after Dad started his station," probably in mid or late September, that DeFord began performing. Programs then were so informal that they were seldom titled and hardly ever even listed in radio schedules as anything more than "local musical programs."

Exum was always looking for promotional devices and gimmicks. Later that fall he came up with the idea of staging musical contests on the air—a radio-age counterpart to the old-time fiddling contests that were currently sweeping the country. Since Nashville seemed to be literally filled with harmonica players, and since the harmonica seemed to be a favorite instrument in Middle Tennessee, Exum decided to stage a harmonica-playing contest on the air. The winner would receive a tube radio set, the runner-up a crystal radio set.

Many of DeFord's white friends—especially a Dr. Grant, whose office was in the building where DeFord was working—urged DeFord to enter. Reluctantly he agreed to. When the day of the contest came, he was surprised to find out that he was the only Black in it. "No Black folks entered because they all knowed I could beat 'em," he said. He wasn't as well known in the white community. At first, none of the contestants objected to his entering, but after they heard him play, several complained that he should have competed with other Blacks, not with whites. Exum held his ground, however, and allowed DeFord to compete. DeFord played one of his train pieces, and a popular hit of the day, "It Ain't Gonna Rain No Mo'." Looking back on the contest, DeFord felt he really outplayed everybody there but sensed that it would not do for Exum to give him the prize. In fact, Exum compromised and gave first prize to a white harp player and the runner-up prize to Bailey, saying that they were "the best of each race." DeFord took his prize, made no objection, and quietly left for home. Later he learned that by doing so he may have avoided serious trouble. Some of the other performers, still not happy with Exum's compromise, were angry that any Black should receive a prize over a white—even if it was the runner-up prize. It frightened DeFord and bothered him; he resolved that he would never again enter contests of this type.

His win brought his first newspaper coverage. In the December 6 issue of the Nashville *Tennessean,* on the "Radio Page," appeared an article about Dad's and the contest:

DAD'S GROWTH IS PHENOMENAL

. . . . Dad says, "Our efforts are to make our friends happy. In addition to the regular musical programs, we are going to put on special frolics from time to time, and during the Christmas season, carol singers every night. Each Wednesday night, the Claude P. Street Piano Co. puts on a classical program and on every Saturday night Dr. Humphrey Bate and his old-time string band entertain.

Another feature that is being looked forward to just at this time is the Old Fiddlers' contest, which will be staged in the near future. The first prize in the French harp contest staged recently was won by J. T. Bland, who played 'Lost John.' The second prize was won by DeFord Bailey, a negro boy, who played 'It Ain't Gonna Rain No Mo'."

DeFord enjoyed playing on the radio and being a part of this rich musical brew. So many amateur musicians were trying to get on the air that Exum and Smith could afford to be selective, taking only the very best for their regulars. DeFord enjoyed hearing good musicians at their best; he seemed to "fit right in."

> They played good music and everything, so I hung around with a whole bunch of them. I was the only Black man in the whole thing, both ways. Didn't no other Black people come around that kind of place. . . . By me being so little, so boyish-looking, why they took up with me, but they didn't take up with Blacks too much at that time. I don't care how good they could play. . . . They just didn't suit them. It wasn't 'cause they was Black. Somehow or other, the style they had didn't fit in, and their ways and things didn't fit in. I was a clean guy, and played with children. . . . I was just like the old folks used to say, "the world's pet."

One of the WDAD regulars was to have an especially large role in DeFord's music. Dr. Humphrey Bate, a genial, fatherly harmonica player, was a respected country doctor from near Castalian Springs, northeast of Nashville, just a county over from where DeFord had grown up. Dr. Bate was also known as the leader of a "string orchestra" that had played all over north-central Tennessee since before the turn of the century. Dr. Bate was almost certainly the first old-time musician to play anything resembling country music over Nashville radio, beginning with his stint at WDAD and later continuing with WSM. Bate was a highly skilled harmonica player himself—he would later make a series of influential records—and he knew just how good DeFord was. As they listened to each other and visited backstage at Dad's, Bate and DeFord built up a mutual respect for each other.

WDAD had the Nashville airwaves to itself for about a month. Then, on October 5, 1925, WSM went on the air in a debut somewhat more auspicious than that of WDAD. Instead of a clutter of second-hand equipment jammed into a second floor over a supply store, WSM could boast of plush studios with thick carpeting, heavy drapes, crystal chandeliers, and a grand piano. Instead of beaming out with 150 watts, its power started up at 1,000 watts, making it one of the two strongest stations in the South, and stronger than 85 percent of all the other stations in the country at the time. Its inaugural program was attended by the governor of Tennessee, the mayor of Nashville, various National Life executives, and some of the leading announcers from stations in Kansas City, Chicago, and Atlanta. The musical

Bailey in the 1930s. Photograph given to Morton by Bailey for use in biography.

entertainment was distinctly upscale: a few light classics, some art songs, selections by local dance bands—but not a note of country or folk music. National Life viewed its station as a cultural service to the people of Nashville and assumed that its audience was the upper middle-class white population who lived in the West End and bought John McCormack records for their expensive Victrolas.

In keeping with this "first-class" image, National Life also went after a nationally known announcer for its station. One of the guests of honor at the October 5 broadcast had been George D. Hay, announcer for WLS in Chicago; Hay had recently been awarded a gold cup by the magazine *Radio Digest* for being voted the most popular announcer in the country. Hay was well known to Tennesseans because, before his stint at Chicago, he had been a well-liked newspaper reporter and radio announcer in Memphis. Though he was an Indiana native, he knew the South and had a keen appreciation for southern culture. Though he was a relatively young man (only thirty in 1925), he cultivated the sobriquet of "the Solemn Old Judge" because of a popular newspaper column he had written in Memphis. Called "Howdy, Judge," it dealt with the goings-on at a local night court, often centering on a dialogue between a white judge and often a Black defendant. National Life made him an offer he couldn't refuse, and on November 2, he arrived in town as "radio director" for WSM.

Though National Life executives didn't know it at the time, Hay also had a fondness for folk music. As a cub reporter in Memphis, he had traveled into Arkansas to attend a country square dance and singing, and found he liked the music; he also began to think about ways to present this kind of homespun culture on the radio. While in Chicago, he became the announcer for a variety program called the *National Barn Dance*, a repertoire company of transplanted southerners and midwesterners who found themselves in the urban environment of Chicago. He was impressed with the widespread appeal that such folk and folklike music had with the radio audience.

When he came to Nashville, he told various people that he wasn't happy with the programming at WSM and that he was going to "start something like the *National Barn Dance* in Chicago," which he "expected to do better because the people [around Nashville] were real and genuine and the people were really playing what they were raised on." Hay was certainly aware of WDAD's patchwork programming that spotlighted old-time music, and he may have been aware that even WSM had broadcasted occasional special programs featuring Dr. Bate, banjoist-singer Uncle Dave Macon, fiddler

Sid Harkreader, and other old-time musicians, programs that had aired even before Hay got to town. Shortly after Hay arrived, on November 28, he aired an impromptu program by Uncle Jimmy Thompson, a champion fiddler from Laguardo, Tennessee. In a scene which has become part of country music's mythology, hundreds of phone calls and telegrams poured in, and Hay suddenly realized that he had an audience for this type of music. On December 27, 1925, WSM sent out a press release saying that "because of the recent revival in the popularity of the old familiar tunes, WSM has arranged to have an hour or two of them every Saturday night, starting December 26." The first "hour or two" featured Thompson and Macon, but soon a larger cast was being assembled for what WSM would shortly dub "The Barn Dance."

One of the first members of this cast was Dr. Humphrey Bate. Hay soon renamed his band the Possum Hunters and made Bate the flagship act of the new show. For a time, Dr. Bate (as well as other musicians) would play on both WDAD and WSM on Saturday nights, casually walking out the door of Dad's station and up the hill about three blocks to WSM. One night Bate asked DeFord to go along with him and play on WSM; DeFord was apprehensive, though, not sure how he would fit in with the fancy new carpets and chandeliers, and begged off. Week after week, though, Bate persisted; finally, one Saturday night (DeFord thought it was after the WDAD harp contest but before Christmas), DeFord ran into Dr. Bate and his daughter (and pianist) Alcyone as they left Dad's on their way up the hill. That night, Bailey recalled, "Dr. Bate wouldn't take no for an answer. . . . They had a hard time getting me to go down there. I was ashamed with my little cheap harp and them with all them fine, expensive guitars, fiddles, and banjos up there. But Dr. Bate told me that 'we're going to take you with us, if we have to tote you.' So I went."

When they arrived at the studio, the show was already in progress. Hay greeted them pleasantly enough but became cool when Bate explained that he wanted DeFord to play on the air. No one should appear, Hay felt, without an audition, and there simply wasn't time for one. Bate persisted. "Judge, I will stake my reputation on the ability of this boy," Alcyone remembered her father saying. Finally the judge relented and let the young harmonica player do a couple of tunes. As he played, Hay fiddled with his wooden steamboat whistle that he used to start and end the show; at the end of the set, Hay was so delighted and amazed that he threw the whistle high into the air. At once he knew he wanted DeFord for the show. "He gave me two dollars and told me to come back next week," DeFord remembered. "'We're going to use you,' he said."

DeFord's first documented appearance in newspaper radio schedules was on June 19, 1926, though he had probably begun regular appearances before then. On the June 19 broadcast, he appeared right after Dr. Bate's segment, doing a fifteen-minute set following Bate's forty-five minutes. Uncle Dave Macon, the nationally known banjoist, was also on the show that night, as well as local fiddle-and-banjo team Lovel & DeMoss and singing announcer Jack Keefe. Curiously, also on the show was a Black gospel group, the Carthage Quartet, from DeFord's native Smith County; they sang spirituals. Whether this was mere coincidence is unknown, but it points up two salient facts about the early Barn Dance. One is that the show, in these early days, was not confined to what would later be called "country music"; the term "old-time music" or "old familiar tunes," which Hay often used to describe the show, encompassed any kind of older music: gospel, brass bands, barbershop quartets, Hawaiian music, even a little jazz. Thus no one was surprised when DeFord played blues on his harp; a far greater restriction was on the age, not the genre, of the repertoire. Judge Hay, for example, expressly forbade him to play the then-popular tune "My Blue Heaven." The second point is that occasionally there were also Blacks on the show in these protean days. Gospel quartets such as the one from Carthage as well as ones from Fisk and a group called the Golden Echo Quartet appeared, as did occasional guitarists and blues singers from Nashville. As the show coalesced around a country music theme, though, such occasional appearances dwindled, and DeFord emerged as the only Black performer on the show after its first couple of years.

Throughout late 1926, DeFord began appearing every week on the Barn Dance, along with other WSM pioneers. These included the Crook Brothers, Lewis and Herman, who led a stringband that featured their twin harmonicas instead of the fiddle as leads; "Dad" Pickard and the Pickard Family, "Dad" being a singer and Jew's harp player who was the show's first singing star and who later went on to network fame; the Binkley Brothers, mild-mannered watch repairmen who played a delightful, lilting fiddle and banjo repertoire; Theron Hale, whose trick fiddling of "The Mocking Bird" won him fame, and His Daughters; and a string trio from Chestnut Mound, the Smith County Trio, who grew up near Carthage not far from DeFord. Judge Hay, who liked to find colorful nicknames for all his performers, dubbed DeFord "the Harmonica Wizard," and thereafter even his radio listing appeared as "DeFord Bailey, the harmonica wizard." Week after week DeFord continued to delight audiences and bring in mail as well as telegrams and phone calls with special requests. One of DeFord's friends who worked in the mailroom told him that his music brought in the first "three-thousand-mile" telegram the station ever received.

One of the very first calls had come in from Thompson's Station, where DeFord's friend and former employer Gus Watson telephoned to say, like a proud parent, that he had "given DeFord his first harmonica."

In the fall of 1927, an incident occurred that was to have far-reaching implications for both DeFord and the Barn Dance. In the spring of that year, the NBC national radio network was formed, with WSM as a member station. This meant that the station could pick up network "feeds" from New York or Chicago and present live concerts by the best-known dance bands and most popular singers. By that fall, there was a lot of talk about the grand opera broadcasts coming out of Chicago, as well as the ongoing *Musical Appreciation Hour* series with noted conductor Dr. Walter Damrosch. Both were carried by WSM, and in December both figured in an event that was to change the name of the Barn Dance. Years later, in his informal memoir *A Story of the Grand Ole Opry,* George Hay wrote this well-known account:

> Judge Hay was in the habit of leaving a studio speaker "on" so he could monitor the closing moments of "The Music Appreciation Hour" being broadcast from the NBC network prior to the WSM Barn Dance. Hay heard the Master of Ceremonies, Doctor Walter Damrosch, introduce a classic work in this fashion:
>
>> While most artists realize that there is no place in the classics for realism, nevertheless, I am going to break one of my rules and present a composition by a young composer from Iowa who sent us his latest number which depicts the on-rush of a locomotive.
>
> Following the composition, the eminent composer-conductor closed his program. Doctor Damrosch's remarks fell on receptive ears in the WSM studio and the Solemn Old Judge, not being above a barbed witticism, opened his Country Music program with this introduction:
>
>> Friends, the program which just came to a close was devoted to the classics. Doctor Damrosch told us that it was generally agreed that there is no place in the classics for realism. However, from here on out for the next three hours, we will present nothing but realism. It will be down to earth for the "earthy."

As if to demonstrate, Hay introduced DeFord Bailey, the crippled harmon-ica player, who executed a highly-descriptive train song called "The Pan American Blues." Judge Hay rubbed additional salt in Doctor Damrosch's wounds by adding, "For the past hour, we have been listening to music largely from Grand Opera, but from now on, we will present "The Grand Ole Opry."

Recent research suggests that this event occurred not on the Saturday night broadcast preceding the regular Barn Dance but on a Wednesday night; whenever a network feed ended on or about 10:00 P.M., it was Hay's habit to have a few old-time musicians on hand for an informal "studio program" until the station signed off. Since he lived in Nashville and was available on short notice, DeFord would have been a logical choice for such duty. Whatever the case, by December the newspapers were referring to the Saturday-night show as "The Grand Ole Opry." Hay liked his spur-of-the-moment witticism and began to apply it to the show in his promotional efforts. And DeFord's music was the direct inspiration for it.

6

"A Gold Mine Walking Around on Earth"

George Hay's decision to change the name of the Barn Dance to the Grand Ole Opry was the capstone to a year of far-reaching promotional activity; whatever might have been Hay's original intention with the show, by 1927 he had decided that he had something of national potential and was setting about to publicize it as best he could, using all of his contacts. This included getting as many people as he could into the recording studios to take advantage of the newly developed fad for "old-time" or "hillbilly" records. Hay himself had appeared on several Columbia pop records in 1925, introducing such WLS acts as Ford & Glenn and dance-band leader Art Kahn. Using his Columbia contacts, he had arranged as early as 1926 to have Uncle Jimmy Thompson recorded, and in April 1927 he set up a session for several WSM artists with Columbia in Atlanta.

DeFord had continued to perform almost every week on the show from mid-1926 to April 1927; radio logs suggest that he was appearing more than any other act, reflecting Hay's enthusiasm for his work. Bailey recalled that Hay came to him during this time one day and exclaimed that DeFord wasn't "nothing but a gold mine walking around on earth." Even on the air Hay was effusive; DeFord never forgot the words he spoke one particular midnight, just as the Opry was closing: "I'm letting you know, DeFord Bailey is the best harp player that was ever knowed out of four hundred years, and still is." According to DeFord, "After he said that, I thought the same thing myself. People didn't tell me that with their mouths, but by coming to see me play. I wondered why they all come to see me and not somebody else. That let me know I must be the best. But I never did take it for granted. God gave that talent for His people. That meant everything."

Given this kind of audience reaction, Hay had no doubt that his young harmonica wizard was a prime candidate for the big talent-hungry record companies.

The time was right. The big New York record companies were just discovering the commercial potential of southern vernacular music, both blues and country. Mamie Smith, whom DeFord had seen at the Bijou, had made the first blues record by a Black artist in 1920; Eck Robertson had recorded the first southern fiddle solo for Victor in 1922, and Fiddlin' John Carson had recorded the first country vocal in 1923 for Okeh. In the months that followed, all the companies rushed to get into the act to tap this new market, and soon talent scouts were beating the bushes across the South looking for fiddlers, banjoists, blues guitarists, and singers. Harmonica records were among the earliest and most popular of the old-time releases; in fact, barely months after Fiddlin' John Carson recorded his "first" country side, his company brought into their New York studios a Virginia mill hand named Henry Whitter. Around December 10, 1923, Whitter recorded three harmonica solos: "Rain Crow Bill Blues," "The Old Time Fox Chase," and "Lost Train Blues (Lost John Blues)." Though Whitter was only an adequate harmonica player, his version of "The Old Time Fox Chase," when issued in March 1924 on Okeh 40029 (see Chapter 7), proved to be one of the company's best-sellers. A similar success occurred two years later, in 1926, when a young Black named Robert "Rabbit Foot" Cooksey recorded a series of harmonica blues with guitar accompaniment for Victor. Cooksey, probably a native of the Southeast who lived and worked in Philadelphia and New York, with his partner Bobby Leecan, recorded pieces like "Black Cat Bone Blues" and "South Street Stomp" and saw them sell well enough to get Cooksey back in the studios no fewer than nine times during 1926 and 1927. The successes of Whitter and Cooksey certainly made the record executives receptive to harmonica music, though as of April 1927, no Black player had actually recorded unaccompanied.

This might explain what happened at DeFord's first attempt to record commercially. Hay had arranged for three of his acts to go to the Columbia session in Atlanta, with the understanding that the records would be issued with the credit line giving the artists' name followed by "Of Radio Station WSM, Nashville, Tennessee." The acts were Obed "Dad" Pickard, a singer and Jew's harp player; the Golden Echo Quartet; and DeFord. Pickard recorded on Thursday, March 31, and then the quartet did four tunes early the following morning. There was only time for DeFord to do two numbers—a large cast of musicians was due in that afternoon to record a skit called "A Fiddler's Convention in Georgia"—and they had him do what was listed in the Columbia logs as "Pan-American Express"

WSM publicity photograph of Bailey. Photograph given to Morton by Bailey for use in biography.

and "Hesitation Mama." DeFord remembered: "We went down on the train to Atlanta one afternoon and came back the next day. They only [recorded] me playing my train and one other tune, 'Hesitation Mama.' Judge wasn't pleased with that. He thought they should have recorded some of my other tunes too, so he decided to cancel the deal and send me to New York instead." Whether the Columbia A&R (artists and repertoire) men were dubious about DeFord's harmonica solos, or whether they were just caught in a time bind, is not known. But the Columbia sides were never issued, and the metal masters were apparently destroyed in a scrap drive during World War II.

Hay swung into action immediately, setting up another session just four-teen days later with the Brunswick-Balke-Collender Company, which issued Brunswick and Vocalion records, in New York. Brunswick was very much aware of the potential for harmonica records and had just tried to lure Robert Cooksey from Victor by recording him under a false name; they were most eager to hear DeFord's stuff. Moreover, just that April the company had inaugurated a new record series, "Songs from Dixie," devoted to old-time southern music, and they were looking for authentic southern talent. DeFord remembered:

It wasn't too much longer 'fore I was off to New York. Mr. Hay arranged everything with somebody from the record company. I think his name was Frank Gaskin. Anyway, I took a train from Nashville to Knoxville, and he met me there. We drove up in a car to Roanoke, Virginia, and caught a train from there on in to New York City.

We got there on Sunday morning. It was Easter Sunday, and we laid 'round the rest of the day in the hotel. Later that week, one morning 'round nine o'clock, we walked up Seventh Avenue to the studio.

They sat me down on a little seat, and showed me three lights on the wall. One light was my signal telling me to get ready, one told me to start, and the last one was the signal to stop playing. I watched the lights and timed my tunes to fit 'em. Each record was three minutes. I stopped right on time for each one. I had played so long, I knowed right when to stop. One time was all it took, since I didn't make a single mistake on none of them. I recorded eight tunes, and I played every one of them perfect the first time. They couldn't get over that. They said I was the first one to ever record in that studio who didn't have to play something more than once. They must have thought that I would have to get warmed up or something, but that's all it took. I didn't need no practice.

After I finished recording the first one, they played it back for me to hear. Then after all of it, I heard the others. I only spent about thirty minutes in the room by myself. It didn't seem like much time. I wasn't tired at all. They let me play whatever I wanted to play. I was getting fifty dollars a side and I decided to give 'em their money's worth. I tried to play my best tunes. That was the first time I had ever played "Fox Chase" for somebody else. Everybody here [in Nashville] didn't know I could play it. They said I set the woods on fire with it. From then on, I had to play it every Saturday night.

The Brunswick files show that DeFord recorded one number, "Pan American Blues," on Monday, April 18, and the bulk of his sides on the following Tuesday, April 19. The eight tunes would eventually constitute his most important and extensive recorded legacy. The other titles, in order, included:

"Dixie Flyer Blues"
"Up Country Blues"
"Evening Prayer Blues"
"Muscle Shoals Blues"
"Old Hen Cackle"
"Alcoholic Blues"
"Fox Chase"

Though the exact sources of these tunes will be discussed later, it is worth noting that, of the eight, two were "train pieces" ("Pan American" and "Dixie Flyer"), two were standards from old-time music ("Fox Chase" and "Old Hen Cackle"), two were up-tempo redactions from vaudeville blues and jazz ("Alcoholic Blues" and "Muscle Shoals Blues"), and two were based on traditional folk melodies ("Evening Prayer" and "Up Country"). All except two were labeled "Blues," though some were in fact not really all that blueslike. Brunswick assumed that the audience for the records was the generally white, old-time music audience, for all but one of the discs were issued in the Brunswick 100 "Songs from Dixie" series—nearly the only records by a Black performer in the series—and four of the sides then issued again in the Vocalion 5000 series, a parallel numerical entitled "Old Time Tunes." According to the trade journal *Talking Machine World,* the first of DeFord's records to be issued was Brunswick 148, "Evening Prayer Blues" and "Alcoholic Blues," in August 1927. In November of that year came Brunswick 146, "Pan American Blues" and "Dixie Flyer Blues." (Brunswick often issued catalog numbers out of sequence.)

In spite of their importance to posterity, the records, DeFord recalled, yielded him little financial benefit at the time:

They were supposed to give me $400 cash money for the eight sides I made for 'em, plus royalties. But I didn't get that much. Judge Hay got 25 percent of the $400 for what he done in arranging for the sessions. Instead of giving me the rest outright, they gave me my share in $10 payments over a period of several months. I finally got $300 in all.

As for the royalty checks, I got three of 'em. The first one was for $80, the second one was for $40, and the third was for $8. Altogether, I got $128 in royalties on the tunes. I was supposed to get 2 percent of each record that sold at 75 cents each. The record sold 15,589 copies in less than six months.

The exact sales of the records have been lost in company files and will probably never be determined with any accuracy. A sale of 15,000, for an old-time music record in 1927, would have been about average, but the fact that the sides were issued on Vocalion, and in one case (Brunswick 147, "Muscle Shoals Blues" and "Up Country Blues") reissued on a later Brunswick coupling in 1930, suggests that the records were moderate commercial successes. Copyright files show that DeFord sought no copyrights on any of his originals from the session, a failure common enough with many old-time and blues musicians of that day and age. But the records had an impact far beyond their immediate royalties: hundreds of harp players, Black and white, learned from them and studied them. And by the end of 1927 other record companies were rushing to record other Black harmonica soloists like Jaybird Coleman (on Gennett), Texan William McCoy (Columbia), Tennesseans Palmer McAbee and El Watson (Victor), and Ollis Martin (Gennett). It is tempting to suggest that DeFord's success on Brunswick, and his continuing popularity on the radio, were at least part of the cause of this activity. Whatever the sales figures, few harmonica players in the early recording industry had as many solo performances issued as did DeFord, and the Brunswick set would constitute a tour de force of southern folk harmonica styles.

Like many old-time musicians before him, DeFord did not like New York. The company provided him with expense money; "they had to," he said, "since I only had 15 cents in my pocket when I left Nashville and I brought that back with me." He did manage to see a little of the town, though:

We stayed in New York for about a week. We was at Thirty-third and Broadway, in the McAlpin Hotel. It cost $6 a day. We stayed on the twenty-second floor. I ate in the hotel and stayed there most of the time, but I walked around some. I went to a place like an arcade, and I bought a belt. You know, three years later that style come down here [to Nashville].

I went down to a subway stop and waited for the subway to stop complete, like a bus does here in Nashville, but it never did. It kept moving slow. I missed two or three before I caught on. I finally got tired of waiting and swung on when them doors opened. Then when I went riding, I got lost. I went to one of them conductors and he told me which car to get on. He told me to stay on 'til I got to Thirty-third and I could see the hotel. I was glad to get off that thing.

Later on, DeFord occasionally joked that "soon as I was done with the recording I went down to the railroad station and asked the ticket agent, 'When's the next train south?' He told me, and I said, 'That is the train I'll be on!'" In reality, he was chaperoned back home by Frank Gaskin, at least

as far as Saltville, Virginia, where we changed trains. He left going in another direction. I got on the next train and it turned out to be the wrong one. I had to change at some place out in the middle of nowhere. It was late at night when I got there and I was there by myself for a long time. After a long time, an old white man come out of the woods and told me I had to flag the train down. He said he'd do it for me. He took a match and lit a piece of paper when he saw the train coming. I'd have missed it if he hadn't been there, 'cause I didn't know nothing about flagging down a train. When that train stopped, I was on it in a flash. I wanted to get home.

Finally I did get home. I got off at the old Tennessee Central Station down at the river. I don't know where all I went, but I was sure glad to get home.

As the Brunswick-Vocalion 78s were released, one at a time, in the summer and fall of 1927, DeFord's fame grew. Next to Uncle Dave Macon, who had been a recording star since 1924, DeFord had more records to his credit than any other early Opry members. Sid Harkreader, Sam and Kirk McGee, Uncle Jimmy Thompson, Dad Pickard, the Golden Echoes—all had made their mark on records by now. Dr. Humphrey Bate was soon set up with a session for Brunswick, making the Opry's two great harmonica players label-mates. With all this activity, it was not too hard for Hay to take the next step and try to lure one of the companies' field recording units into setting up shop in Nashville. He succeeded in the fall of 1928; Victor had made Memphis into a regular center for blues recording, and the company was planning an especially long session in September. They agreed to stop off in Nashville after they were finished and en route to their next major session in Atlanta. Hay at once began lining up more of his early Opry artists; he made sure DeFord was on the list.

The scene was thus set for DeFord's third commercial recording session. It was to be historic in at least one sense: it was the first recording session held in what would become Music City USA. The Victor engineers—headed by their ace A&R man Ralph Peer, who just the year before had discovered country greats the Carter Family and Jimmie Rodgers at just such a field session in Bristol, Tennessee—set up their gear on September 28. The location was the YMCA building that had formerly housed National Life offices, just across the street from the WSM studios. Almost all the early Opry acts who had not yet signed with a major company were scheduled for the session: the Binkley Brothers Dixie Clodhoppers with vocalist Jack Jackson, Paul Warmack & His Gully Jumpers, Theron Hale & His Daughters, Ed Poplin's Old-Time Band, the Crook Brothers' stringband, and the blind fiddler Joe Mangrum. DeFord knew all of them.

Later fans of DeFord would claim that he was the first to record at this session, and thus the first artist to record in Nashville. The Victor files, however, show that he recorded third, after the Binkley Brothers and the Gully Jumpers. DeFord did his session at about 2:00 P.M. on October 2; according to the engineer's logs, he did eight numbers in four and a half hours, ending at 6:30. Two takes were done of each tune—a standard practice in those days in case one of the fragile wax masters was damaged in shipment back to New York. The tunes, all different from those in the Brunswick sessions, included:

"Lost John"
"John Henry"
"Ice Water Blues"
"Kansas City Blues"
"Casey Jones"
"Wood Street Blues"
"Davidson County Blues"
"Nashville Blues"

DeFord recalled that, during the version of "John Henry," an accident caused him to have to re-do the piece. "I was blowing my brains out and that car horn went 'blah!' It messed me up. I knowed that tune wasn't no 'count. They had a window up. I couldn't understand that."

Victor was ahead of other record companies of the time in checking out copyrights on the selections it recorded; the Victor session sheets show that DeFord claimed authorship of three of the tunes: "Ice Water Blues," "Wood Street Blues" (DeFord was then living at 908 Wood Street), and "Davidson County Blues." Of the three, only the latter was ever to be actually copyrighted by DeFord, on June 3, 1929, for Peer's company, Southern Music. "Kansas City Blues" was attributed to blues songster Jim Jackson, while the balance were considered "public domain." For some reason, however, only three of the eight sides were ever released by Victor: "Ice Water Blues," coupled with "Davidson County Blues," appeared on one release; "John Henry," coupled with harmonica solos by other artists, appeared on two others. Unlike Brunswick, Victor released the double coupling in their "race" series aimed at Black audiences; there it jostled with jazz records by Duke Ellington and Jelly Roll Morton as well as various blues and gospel releases. It apparently sold fairly well and was subsequently reissued on Victor's subsidiary labels, Bluebird and Sunrise. In fact, the Bluebird issue of "Davidson County" and "Ice Water" guaranteed the disc would stay in print years longer than the average old-time or blues 78 in those days. The Bluebird catalog, which combined the earlier race and hillbilly series into one series, featured DeFord's record in its first issue, of June 1936, almost eight years after its original recording date.

"John Henry" didn't fare as well. The tune was a favorite of WSM listeners, and when he played it on the air, DeFord would wear two steel bars in a rack around his neck and hit the bars with a hammer in time to the music, imitating the steel hammer in the song. But for some reason, Victor did not issue it until the spring of 1932, and then they issued it in both the "Old Time" and the blues series. On the blues series it was backed by another harmonica solo, by Noah Lewis, a member of the Memphis Jug Band; on the "Old Time" series, it was backed by a solo by white harmonica player D. H. Bilbro. By the time the record was issued in both series, the Depression had wrecked phonograph record sales, and Victor files suggest that each release sold fewer than four hundred copies. As a result, "John Henry," in either coupling, became the rarest of the DeFord Bailey records; some collectors think there exists today only one copy of each original release.

DeFord never knew what the other musicians received from their participation in the first historic Nashville session, but he got a lump-sum payment of $200, which was sent to him in early 1929. In truth, the Nashville session of 1928 was hardly a success. Out of the sixty-nine recordings made that week, only thirty-six were ever issued by Victor in the form of 78s. This was a much higher casualty rate than for other similar field sessions, and nobody seems to know why so many of the sides were not issued. DeFord's three out of eight was a good percentage compared to some artists. It is possible that the recording machine was somehow malfunctioning, producing inferior masters; or there might not have been enough "original" material to suit Victor; or Hay might have became irate at the company and blocked releases, as he had with DeFord's first Columbia recordings. Recent searches of the Victor vaults have failed to uncover any of the unreleased masters DeFord cut, and it is likely that they are lost to history.

Thus, in one eighteen-week period in 1927 and 1928, DeFord made what would turn out to be his entire output of commercial recordings. They totaled eleven sides—barely enough for a modern LP. Even though they represented some of the finest harmonica playing ever captured on disc, they brought DeFord little reward, and he never again sought seriously to get into a recording studio. Scratchy, fragile, hard to get, these few old 78s remain today our only real evidence of how DeFord sounded in his prime, and why so many musicians and fans were fascinated by his music. Though the three Victor sides have periodically been brought back into print in the LP age, the exuberant Brunswick efforts have never been reissued in any authorized form on any domestic LP. Fans from as far away as Germany and England exchange tapes of the old records, studying the eleven sides and wondering just how well they reflect DeFord's larger radio and concert repertoire.

7

"Them Songs"

There are very few recordings and very few detailed printed programs either of DeFord's prime years on the Grand Ole Opry or of his many concert appearances on tour with Opry groups. Unlike many other country stars, he published no "souvenir songbooks" of his favorite pieces. As we have seen, his recorded legacy consists of eleven three-minute performances, in contrast to the hundred-plus recordings of his contemporaries on the Opry such as Uncle Dave Macon or the Delmore Brothers. To get a sense of his repertoire, therefore, we must rely on his own memories of tunes he liked to play or still continued to play in the 1970s. Fortunately, DeFord had a keen appreciation of tunes and was quick to give credit to his sources. He was always eager to learn new material, and he was still creating new pieces in the 1970s. He learned "some of them from Black folks and some from white folks"; he "picked 'em up" whenever he traveled; "if I heard it and liked it, then it was mine," he said.

The song list in the Appendix is an attempt to compile a working repertoire of DeFord's tunes. Not all were harmonica tunes; some he played on the guitar, and a few (such as "Lost John") on the banjo. Some he recorded during my interviews; others he just talked about.

The oldest of these tunes were ones DeFord learned as a child back in Smith County. These belong to the "Black hillbilly" music of his grandfather and uncles. It is important to remember that, during his first ten years, DeFord saw much of his grandfather Lewis Bailey, the champion fiddle player, since Lewis lived with DeFord's branch of the family. At least some of Lewis's fiddle-tune repertoire was passed on to DeFord, who promptly converted the tunes to harmonica numbers. One of these appeared on DeFord's Victor session as "Ice

Water Blues." He knew it was one of his grandfather's fiddle tunes but forgot Lewis's name for it and made up the "Ice Water" title. Blues historian Paul Oliver has suggested that the melody is based on the old 1904 pop song "The Preacher and the Bear," which was widely known in traditional music, but it also resembles an old Middle Tennessee fiddle tune called "Trace Chains," which is still played in the area today. "Ice Water Blues" continued to appeal to DeFord as he grew older, but it became more difficult to play because in later years he lost many of his teeth. He recalled that when he recorded the tune (in 1928) "I had all my teeth. I had gold all across here. . . . See, I was working for a dental supply house on Eighth and Church. And Miller—he's dead now—I had my shop by his office one time. I picked out my own teeth and helped fix 'em myself . . . and put 'em on all across here with gold. That's when I made that record. My teeth and mouth was in good shape. . . . I could blow them things in odd places where I get them keen notes at." Other songs from this tradition that DeFord retained included "Old Hen Cackle," "The Fox Chase," "John Henry," "Lost John," "Old Joe Clark," and "Comin' 'Round the Mountain." DeFord said: "All them old songs was here before I come into the world. . . . My grandpa played 'em when I was a little boy. I learned 'em all."

There were other tunes from his childhood that he did not regularly play on the Opry but that he had stored in his memory and occasionally played for variety when they came to mind. One was a beautiful tune called "Sweet Marie," a fiddle piece his grandfather played. "It was a waltz piece," he remembered. "It had a good sound." "Alberta, Don't Grieve about a Dime" was learned from his uncle George Reedy, who played it on the guitar when DeFord was very young. It too, he recalled, "was kind of like a waltz." "Sally Sittin' in a Saucer" was taken from a schoolyard game and song played by children when DeFord was growing up, while "Whoa, Mule, Whoa" he learned when he was nine years old from an old Black man, Jim McCarver, who lived on a nearby farm. Another early song was "Has the Cat Got the Whoopin' Cough and the Dog Got the Measles," a surrealistic and funny song that was made into a hit record in 1929 by hillbilly singer Walter "Kid" Smith.

Once he left Smith County and moved into the Middle Tennessee–Nashville area, DeFord began to pick up newer songs from the pop, blues, and vaude-ville circuits of the day. He picked up "Hesitation Mama," one of the first two numbers he recorded in his ill-fated Columbia session, when he was fifteen and living in Franklin. Though he continued to keep the tune, which is better known as "Hesitation Blues," in his repertoire for years (it became a standard with him), and often performed it on the harmonica, he knew lyrics to it:

Wake up mama, don't you sleep too late,
When your good man calls you, don't you hesitate,
Hello central, give me 99,
I can call up a doctor on the telephone,
How long will I have to wait?

I ain't no doctor, but I'm a doctor's son,
I can ease your pain 'til the doctor comes,
Tell me how long,
Can I see you when I want to,
No, you got to hesitate.

The most familiar version of "Hesitation Blues" was published and copyrighted in 1915 by "Father of the Blues" W. C. Handy; this, too, is the version on several Victrola records around 1916 (cf. the "hit" version by Prince's orchestra, Columbia 5772) as well as the basis for several vaudeville blues recordings later in the 1920s. However, DeFord's version has little in common with Handy's text; aside from the similarity of the "hello central" idea, the two have no other related lines. It is possible that DeFord picked up a folk variant of Handy's tune bare months after Handy published, but it is more likely that DeFord picked up a variant of the traditional version of the song that Handy based his composition on.

In Nashville in the early 1920s DeFord was suddenly exposed to a smorgasbord of musical styles and sources. "It Ain't Gonna Rain No Mo'," with which DeFord won his WDAD radio contest, was a major record hit in 1923, as sung by a ukulele-playing Chicago vaudevillian named Wendell Hall, known as "the Red-Headed Music Maker." The song was actually based on a much older folk tune known both to whites and to Blacks in Middle Tennessee. In a book that came out in 1922, a year before Hall's recording, Nashville-based Black folklorist Thomas Talley had even published a version of it that he had heard around 1915. DeFord liked the song, and it became a standard in his repertoire, remaining there until his death. From a Black piano player who worked at the Bijou Theater, DeFord learned "Cow Cow Blues," which he would rename "Davidson County Blues" on his Victor recording. "I picked it up by working in a theater. Some Black man was playing it on a piano while the untalkable picture was goin' on.

You know, the picture didn't have no sound then and he played along with it. He played music for the picture. I liked the tune and picked it up." The piano player had probably learned it from Charles "Cow Cow" Davenport, the blues and jazz piano player who made the piece famous; Davenport, in fact, routinely played Nashville on the T.O.B.A. circuit.

Also at the Bijou were the great "classic blues" singers DeFord admired so much. He especially remembered Bessie Smith, generally considered the greatest of classic blues singers, and from her live shows learned "Muscle Shoals Blues" and "Up Country Blues." The latter he learned one memorable night when he actually opened a show for Bessie. "She came through with her show, and they had me play down there before she came on," he recalled. "That woman could really sing. She had a good band, too." In fact, one of the local radio stations broadcast that program, but DeFord doesn't remember whether it was WSM. He did remember that he visited with Smith backstage, and that after he played his harmonica solos, she came out and sang one song, letting folks know she would be on later that night. At that point, he decided to go home so he could hear how she sounded on the radio. "When I done my part, I went home so I could turn my radio on and hear her and see how she sounded. I wasn't interested in listening at her there on the stage. I was interested in listening at her on the air. She could sing, too. Regular old blues. 'Gulf Coast Blues,' 'Rattlesnake Blues,' all them blues. . . . Just open her mouth and let it come."

Both "Muscle Shoals Blues," which Judge Hay singled out as one of DeFord's "hit numbers" on the Opry, and "Up Country Blues" had been composed by a Texas writer, George W. Thomas. Though DeFord learned both from Bessie Smith's vaudeville show, Smith herself never recorded either one. "Muscle Shoals" had been recorded by Lizzie Miles (in 1922) and Edith Wilson (1924) while "Up [the] Country Blues" had been recorded by Tiny Franklin (1923) and Sippie Wallace (1923). DeFord's harmonica adaptation of both tunes was uniquely different from the originals.

Other tunes DeFord acquired were more pop or jazz. In 1928, when in Knoxville, Tennessee, he began playing "Get Out and Get under the Moon," which had been made into popular records by bandleader Paul Whiteman and by singer Helen Kane. DeFord remembered that he had heard the tune before but didn't work it up until late 1928; at the time he was sitting in his room, where he had a piano, and he tried to play the song on the harp as well as on the piano, finally deciding on the harp. On another occasion, when Bailey was twenty-three, he actually "bought" a tune for a nickel. He was riding his bicycle down South Street in Nashville when he heard a Black man playing a song on a guitar and harp. Since he had heard only part of it, he told the man he would give him a nickel if he would play it again. The man did, and, as DeFord said, "I had it from then on." The song was "Gotta See Mama Every Night," and though neither DeFord nor his informant knew it at the time, it had been written in 1923 by vaudeville figure Billy Rose and recorded in the same year by several jazz and blues singers.

Only occasionally would DeFord pick up tunes from other Opry performers. One performer whose songs he liked was Obed "Dad" Pickard, the singer from Ashland City, Tennessee, whose knowledge of old songs helped him win network fame with his singing family. One song that DeFord began using was Pickard's version of an old fiddle tune: "He had a lot of songs I liked," recalled DeFord, "but I only took up with one. That was 'Little Sallie Gooden.'"

DeFord often listened to the records of Bessie Smith, Mamie Smith, Jim Jackson, and others. They had a different "whang" to their music, and he liked it. (Until he was in his seventies, he thought Bessie, Clara, and Mamie Smith, three of the most prolific blues singers to record, were "all each others' sisters.") One song learned from records was "Shake That Thing," which he featured often on the Opry:

Old Uncle Jack was a jelly roll king,
He got a hump in his back from shakin' that thing,
I got to shake that thing,
I got to shake that thing,
Oh, shake that thing.

This was taken from a popular 1925 Paramount record by Papa Charlie Jackson, a veteran Black songster called by historians the first commercially successful self-accompanied bluesman. Though details of his life are unknown, he seems to have based many of his songs on older minstrel, vaudeville, and medicine-show styles. Accompanied by a six-string banjo-guitar, he recorded original versions of blues standards like "Salty Dog Blues," "Spoonful," and "Sliding Delta." His records were also direct influences on Sam and Kirk McGee, the famed white duo that shared Opry stages with DeFord, and Jackson also recorded "The Cat's Got the Measles," which Bailey also had in his repertoire.

Another Jackson was also an important influence on DeFord through records. This was Mississippi singer Jim Jackson (1884–1937), no relation to Papa Charlie, whose recordings of "Kansas City Blues" and "Hey Mama—It's Nice Like That" were prized items in DeFord's collection. Jackson was one of the oldest songsters to record in the 1920s; his repertoire consisted of dozens of songs he had learned, refashioned, or made up during years as a traveling medicine-show musician. From 1915 to 1930 he traveled throughout the South, including Nashville, playing his distinctive heavy strum guitar style and singing his songs. For many years he lived in Memphis, where he played on Beale Street—a fact DeFord was aware of. (DeFord did not recall ever meeting Jackson, but he might well have seen him at one of the medicine shows he attended in Edgehill in the early 1920s.) Jackson possibly learned "Kansas City Blues" from another singer-guitarist from his hometown, Hernando, Mississippi; whatever the case, he had already made the song a favorite on the medicine-show circuit long before he recorded it for Vocalion in October 1927. The record, whose two sides were labeled "Jim Jackson's Kansas City Blues, Part 1" and "Part 2," became one of the best-selling country blues records in history. Within a month after its release, Jackson was called back into the studio to do a follow-up, "Jim Jackson's Kansas City Blues, Parts 3 and 4," in early 1928; eventually he did yet a third follow-up, issued as "I'm Gonna Move to Louisiana, Parts 1 and 2."

DeFord played "Kansas City Blues" both on harmonica and on guitar but usually the latter; he would also sing verses. It became one of his best remembered pieces; he often performed it (as a vocal) on the Opry, and friends like Sam McGee never tired of praising "DeFord's bull-dog song." DeFord also continued to perform the song in his rare public performances in later life, during the 1970s. Like most blues, the lyrics changed slightly each time he played it, but he generally sang it as follows:

1. My Mama told me, Daddy told me too,
   Everybody grinning in your face ain't no friend to you.
   You ought to move to Kansas City.
   I'm gonna move, babe,
   Out where they can't find me.

2. I wish I was a catfish, just swimming in the sea,
   Had some good woman, fishing after me,
   I'd swim to Kansas City, where they can't find me,
   I'm gonna move, babe,
   Out where they can't find me.

3. Don't you like my peaches, don't you shake my tree,
   Get out of my orchard, let my peaches be,
   We're gonna move to Kansas City,
   I'm gonna move, babe,
   Out where they can't find me.

4. I feel like jumping from the treetop to the ground,
   'Cause the girl I love don't want me hanging around,
   I'm gonna move to Kansas City,
   I'm gonna move, babe,
   Out where you can't find me.

5. Don't pay no attention 'bout the mule being poor,
   Put him in a stable and feed him some more,
   He'll move to Kansas City,
   I'm gonna move to Kansas City,
   Out where you can't find me.

6. I got me a bulldog, shepherd, and two greyhounds,
   Two high yellers, one black and one brown,
   I'm gonna move to Kansas City,
   I'm gonna move, babe,
   Out where they don't want you.

7. I got to start walking, my feet get soaking wet,
   I got to think about my good girl, I ain't quit walking yet,
   I'm gonna move to Kansas City,
   I'm gonna move, babe,
   Out where they can't find me.

8. You can see the ocean, so long, deep, and wide,
   I can see my good girl standing on the other side,
   I'm gonna move to Kansas City,
   I'm gonna move, babe,
   Out where they can't find me.

A comparison of DeFord's version with the original Jim Jackson recordings reveals some interesting rearrangements. DeFord's stanzas 1 and 6 come from "Part 1" of the Vocalion record; stanzas 3 and 8 are drawn from the other Vocalion side, "Part 2." But then stanza 2 comes from Jackson's sequel record, "Part 3," and stanza 4 comes from its flip side, "Part 4." DeFord's stanzas 5 and 7 apparently come from Jackson's second sequel, 'I'm Gonna Move to Louisiana." It thus seems likely that DeFord had all three of Jim Jackson's records and extracted from them the stanzas he thought best suited his own needs, his own audience, or the dictates of the early Grand Ole Opry. Some of the stanzas he omitted have references to specific places—Beale Street, Memphis, Jackson (Mississippi), and the like—references with which Bailey and his audience might not have had any direct association. The stanzas DeFord retained do share a certain consistency, with their references to animals and fish, and his redaction of the song has more coherence than Jackson's original.

Religious songs also formed a part of the Bailey repertoire. DeFord was brought up in the Methodist Church, where he learned many old-time gospel songs; he tried out virtually all of these on his harmonica. When he began playing regularly on the Opry, it seemed natural for him to include one or more of them in his segment of the program. Ones that emerged as favorites with him included "Good News," "Gonna Eat at the Welcome Table Some of These Days," "Cry Holy unto the Lord," "Old Time Religion," "Swing Low, Sweet Chariot," "In the Sweet Bye and Bye," and "When the Saints Go Marching In."

In addition to playing the old familiar gospel standards, DeFord created at least one religious tune of his own. This was "Evening Prayer Blues," recorded for Brunswick, and a special favorite of Judge Hay. In it DeFord "imitates" a powerful preacher leading his congregation in prayer; the model for the style was a famous Nashville preacher of the 1930s, Zema W. Hill, whom DeFord heard a number of times. Hill, also the owner of a local funeral home, made a big impression on young DeFord. "He was a good man. He buried many a people whether or not they had any money. He buried 'em right on. Put you away nice. I learned a whole lot off him—preaching, prayer. He was a good preacher."

Like many blues performers, when he sang lyrics DeFord saw the words as a type of dramatic expression rather than as sheer autobiography. In spite of his fondness for "Kansas City Blues," for instance, he never seriously considered moving to that city. He often sang an old 1919 pop song, "Alcoholic Blues"—"one of them Smith girls' tunes"—that included the following lines:

I got the blues, I got the blues,
I got the alcoholic blues,
I got the blues, Tallahassee,
I got the blues, Tallahassee.

This occasionally bothered him, for everybody who knew DeFord knew that he was a devout teetotaler. By the same token, he was a family man with a stable lifestyle during the time he sang his "Howling Blues":

Sometimes I feel like howling,
Just like a wolf dog,
I got the howling blues,
I don't know what to do,
Sometimes I feel like howling,
Just as loud as I can.

When you see me walking,
And talking to myself,
I got the blues,
I don't know what to do,
When you see me howling,
I got the blues.

Sometimes I wonder
Just what's gonna become of me,
I feel like howling,
Just like a howling wolf dog.

Well, I'm gonna trot on away from here,
And I won't be back no more,
Sometimes I feel like walking,
Hey, by myself,
I got the blues,
I don't know what to do.

However, if the occasion called for it, DeFord could create or adapt a blues that did have a specific personal meaning. When I was living in Texas, DeFord made plans to visit me; reluctant to fly, he planned to make the trip on a Greyhound bus and forged the following blues for my benefit.

Greyhound Blues

I'm going to catch a Greyhound,
    And leave this great big town,
I'm going to catch a Greyhound,
    And leave this great big town.
I want to tell you one thing,
    Leave this driving to us,
I'm going to catch a Greyhound,
    And ride it nationwide,
If you want to take a trip,
Why don't you go Greyhound?

I'm going to catch a Greyhound,
    And won't be back no more,
I'm going to catch a Greyhound,
    And step over in Dallas, Texas,
I'm going to leave this town,
    And won't be back no more.

I'm going to catch a Greyhound,
    And go to Beaumont, Texas,
        Diddle da da,
Going down to Texas where them
    Rattlesnakes grow,
Where they're crawling in the sun,
    Shining like a diamond ring,
Well, I got the Greyhound blues,
    But I don't know what to do,
I feel like walking.

Though best known for his harmonica playing, DeFord was a more than adequate blues singer and guitarist, often performing this way both on Opry broadcasts and at concerts. The only surviving examples of his singing come from informal tapes and concert recordings, none of which have thus far been made public. In general, however, Bailey seems to have done with blues what many of the other early Opry singers did with Anglo-American songs: he borrowed from both pop and folk sources, stylizing and adapting these songs to tailor them to the large, wide-based radio audience. The McGee Brothers, the Delmore Brothers, and others would later bring Anglo-Americanized versions of the blues to the Opry stage, but DeFord's link to the form was earlier, more direct, and more potent. "The blues is a sad music," he noted:

It ain't nothing but you're hard up and can't do nothing for yourself. Like when you're way away from home and try to make it home and can't. Or got children and they're sick and you can't feed 'em and feel bad. Almost like a church song. Real serious. Like you're sick and don't know what to do for your family. You go to singing. Calling on the Lord to help. We call it the blues.

When all was said and done, though, it was a set of three imitation pieces that were to become the most famous tunes in the Bailey repertoire. These were "The Fox Chase," "Pan American Blues," and "Dixie Flyer Blues." All three had been recorded at his Brunswick session, but it was their performance over WSM that endeared them to a huge national audience and permanently associated them with DeFord.

Though DeFord had known "The Fox Chase" since his youth, he didn't play it on the Opry until after he recorded it in 1927. By the 1930s, the WSM News Service described the piece as "one of his most famous creations." It included "the sound of the fox-howls, the barking dogs, and the huntsman's call to the hounds at the same time." To the Opry's rural audience, many of whom still engaged in fox hunting and field trials for their dogs, the effect was vastly appealing; DeFord was almost forced to play it every time he appeared. Fans who saw him play the tune in person were even more amazed at how he played it: he would actually remove the harp several inches from his mouth, while playing it, yet keep the chase going without a break. Over the years he continued to add new sounds and effects to this already remarkable creation.

Neither DeFord nor his Opry fans knew just how deep the roots of the "Fox Chase" were. The performing style itself—especially its mixture of overblowing and whooping-has been called by one scholar "pure wordless reminiscence of . . .

Bailey holding a harmonica and a photograph of the Pan American Express.
Photograph given to Morton by Bailey for use in biography.

African ancestry" and seems to have been a part of Black folk music since the late 1870s. The blues composer W. C. Handy, in his autobiography, remembers some of his earliest musical experiences while growing up in northwest Alabama in the late 1870s: "Sometimes we were fortunate enough to have a French harp on which we played the fox and hounds and imitated the railroad trains—harmonica masterpieces." Yet the melodic fragments of "The Fox Chase," and the very idea of recreating a fox chase on an instrument, seems to have its source in Irish bagpipe music. Irish pipers even today still play a "Fox Chase" on their bellows-blown Uilleann pipes, which are made in such a way as to enable the player to bend notes and alter tones much in the manner of a blues harp player. Many pipers consider "The Fox Chase" to be the creation of a famous blind piper named Edward Keating Hyland, who performed it before King George IV in 1821. It was published in *O'Farrell's Pocket Companion for the Irish or Union Pipes*. Like many Irish piping tunes, it was probably adapted to the fiddle in later years and made its way into America during the waves of Irish immigration before the Civil War. Early recordings of fiddle music from the South contain a number of "Fox Chases," and many Tennessee fiddlers learned a version popularized by the state's well-known fiddling governor, Alf Taylor. It is quite likely that DeFord's grandfather, contest champion Lewis Bailey, played his "Fox Chase" on the fiddle; DeFord certainly included the tune among the "old-time" ones he brought from Smith County, and this might have explained his initial reluctance to play it on the Opry.

As noted in Chapter 6, a harmonica version of "The Fox Chase" first appeared on record in late 1923 when a white Virginia mill hand, Henry Whitter, recorded "The Old Time Fox Chase" for Okeh Records. Though Whitter copyrighted the piece, and though his later publicity gave him credit for there "hardly ever" being "a Saturday night without a fox chase . . . on the radio," he was almost certainly adapting a piece that was already well entrenched in both Black and white traditions. Whitter left no statements as to where he learned the piece, but it is similar in structure and melody to the one DeFord later used. The main difference between Whitter's performance and Bailey's is one of technical ability; DeFord is able to articulate the fast melodic sequence (the B part) much better than Whitter did, and he makes the wailing "call" at the start of the piece much richer and more complex. However, Whitter's version preceeded DeFord's record by some three years—Whitter's Okeh record came out in March 1924, DeFord's Brunswick version in the summer of 1927—and it achieved wide popularity. In fact, at Victor's famous Bristol session in 1927, Whitter rerecorded his version for the better recording machines, and in 1929 he did a "Fox Chase No. 2" for Victor in Memphis. Later

Poster of Dixie Flyer route and schedule. Illustration courtesy of CSX Transportation.

reissues on Bluebird kept Whitter's record in print and before the public well into the mid-1930s. DeFord had one advantage Whitter never had, however: regular appearances on a major radio show. Thus DeFord's version of "Fox Chase" was the source and inspiration for many later ones, including that of Sonny Terry, who would later tour with Woody Guthrie and popularize the tune to a new generation. Dozens of harp players, Black and white, also recorded their versions of the tune. Harmonica historian Michael S. Licht has identified some thirty-nine variants of the piece recorded either by commercial companies or the Library of Congress between 1923 and 1977. It is not surprising that, as DeFord made occasional guest appearances on the Opry's "Old Timers' Nights" in the 1970s, he was invariably asked to play "The Fox Chase."

His other most requested pieces were his two train pieces, "Pan American Blues" and "Dixie Flyer Blues." Each of these is a tour de force of DeFord's rich bag of techniques; each duplicates the sound of a high-speed locomotive, and each lets the listener follow a steam engine as it starts off sluggishly, quickly picks up speed, highballs it down the track, and finally loses itself in the distance, its whistle echoing away. Yet the pieces are not mere imitations; hundreds of other harmonica players were adept at that. DeFord's genius lay in his ability to arrange these sounds into a complex musical form, to integrate them with snatches of melody and harmony. The results were spectacular; they captured the imagination of the Opry audiences for years.

The train was a major image in early country music. From the very first country hit record, "The Wreck of the Old 97" in 1924, through dozens of other songs like "Casey Jones," "Engine 143," "Railroad Bill," and the many train songs of Jimmie Rodgers, railroad songs dominated the music's first decade. A 1981 study by folklorist Norm Cohen *(Long Steel Rail: The Railroad in American Folksong)* has documented no fewer than eighty-five major railroad songs from the early years of country music, some recorded as many as twenty times. By the 1920s, the train had become a multifaceted symbol for millons of rural Americans, who saw the train as a romantic symbol for what lay beyond the isolated farms and lonely small towns. The early Opry had numerous connections to the railroads; performers like Jack Jackson and fiddler Arthur Smith, as well as several announcers, had actually worked on the railroad and in some cases continued to do so even though they were also performing on the early shows. Many artists took the train into Nashville every Saturday for their shows. Early Opry favorites included songs like Sam McGee's "Railroad Blues" (in which he actually imitated DeFord's harmonica on his guitar) and Dad Pickard's "Little Red Caboose behind the Train." Later, of course, the Opry itself would become closely associated with Roy Acuff's famous "Wabash Cannonball."

DeFord had become fascinated by the train at an early age. On the farm in Smith County he could hear the train passing some five miles to the south, and he at once knew it was different from any of the other sounds he heard on the farm. It soon became a challenge to duplicate that sound on his harp. "I was playing the train long before I ever saw one," he remembered. It was not until he was nine

Dixie Flyer at Union Station in Nashville. Photograph courtesy of CSX Transportation.

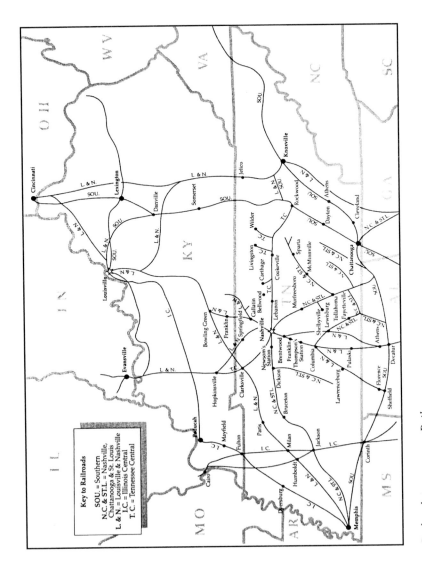

Railroads important to Bailey.

years old, and moving from Smith County, that he saw his first train and had his first train ride (see Chapter 3).

At Newsom's Station, his family lived much nearer the railroad than they had in Smith County. Located just a few miles west of Nashville, they didn't have to wait until the "wind was just right" to hear the train clearly; now they were so close they could set their clocks by it, as DeFord recalled:

> I lived close to a train, I guess about two miles, almost . . . down in Newsom's Station. I lived back in a hollow there. This man had such a big farm that the railroad almost split his farm. We'd go down across the railroad to pick beans, pull corn, and things like that for dinner, you know.
>
> A train'd come along, maybe a freight or maybe a passenger. That passenger'd come along about three o'clock every day. I'd watch that train. I could hear that one at home. I knowed what time it run and I'd listen at it. It had a pretty sound on it. A pretty brass bell.

When DeFord and his foster brothers and sisters went to school at Newsom's Station, he had a chance to hear the train close up. Every day they would pass under a low train trestle just as one of the fast-moving trains, the Dixie Flyer, came through. The Dixie Flyer was an express train on the Nashville, Chattanooga, and St. Louis line (the so-called "Dixie Line"); advertisements of the time trumpeted that "the Dixie Flyer route" was the "solid train between Chicago-St. Louis and Florida"; every day it came down from Chicago through Evansville, Indiana, and Nashville on its way to Jacksonville, Florida.

> I'd go to school the next morning and that Dixie Flyer was coming in from California. I'd meet that train every morning at eight o'clock. I'd leave on time to meet it. Sometime after the man, the motorman, seen what I was doing, he'd blow round the corner to see if I was there. He'd blow that whistle at me—two longs and two shorts. He'd do that every day.
>
> I'd run and get under the trestle. I'd hold my head down and put something over my eyes to keep cinders out of my eyes. Me and my foster sister would do that. We'd listen to the sound, and then I'd play that sound all the way to school.

On July 9, 1918, shortly before DeFord left for Nashville, Newsom's Station was the scene of one of the worst train wrecks in American history. The same

Dixie Flyer that DeFord watched so closely was involved in a two-train collision that killed 101 people. It made a lasting impression on the young harmonica player. Years later he talked about it often, seeing it as a sign both of God's providence and of the fact that trains, no matter how exciting and appealing, had their limitations.

When he moved to Franklin and later to Thompson's Station, the young DeFord found that another railroad line, the Louisville & Nashville (L&N), was nearby. At Thompson's Station, the family's small wooden farmhouse was less than a mile from the tracks, and the sounds would come clearly across the rolling hills. These too he listened for, and these too he tried to duplicate.

Of all the musicians who have played train pieces through the years, it is doubtful that any spent more time developing their train sounds than DeFord did.

> I worked on my train for years, getting that train down right. I caught that train down just like I wanted in a matter of time. I got the engine part. Then I had to make the whistle.
>
> It was about, I expect, seventeen years to get that whistle. It takes time to get this stuff I'm talking about, original. You don't get no original stuff like this in a day or two. It takes years to get it down piece by piece. I got that whistle so it would have a double tone to it, a music tone.
>
> And when cattle was on the track and all that kind of thing, how to make a scary or distressed blow. Then I knowed how to make a harp sound like it was going over a trestle or a deep curve. Like when you in the mountains and going through a tunnel. I could blow like that; and like when you going through a tunnel, you might meet someone, like a person.
>
> I done all that kind of stuff when I was a boy; I'd listen to everything.

The results of all this were certainly more than a couple of pieces of casual imitation or "novelty" harp playing, as DeFord himself was keenly aware; he became a sort of connoisseur of train pieces.

> Some people can play the train, but they can't make it move like I do. Most of theirs sound like they're running, but the sound is standing in one place too long.
>
> You can tell my train is moving. Every time I blow, you can tell I'm getting further. It's moving out of sight as I blow. The sound of their train is moving, but staying in sight too long. I'm always reaching out. When I get about 115 miles an hour, I can feel it. My normal speed is ninety-five

miles an hour. That don't feel like I'm doing nothing, but my train sure enough moves along.

It was the famous fiddler Clayton McMichen, with whom DeFord toured briefly in the mid-1930s, that told him his train was moving at ninety-five miles an hour. "His car was in key with my 'A' harp," according to DeFord. "One night he was out on the road late, driving ninety-five miles an hour coming into Nashville, and heard me blowing my train on the radio. When he got there, he told me I was blowing in time with his Packard at ninety-five miles an hour."

When DeFord got his train down "pretty good," he asked one of his foster sisters what to call it. She told him to name it after the Pan American Express, "since it was the fastest around." The Pan American was a deluxe L&N passenger flyer that ran daily between Cincinnati and New Orleans, stopping at Louisville, Nashville, and Birmingham. It was inaugurated in 1921, quickly became popular, and DeFord saw it often as it passed through Union Station in Nashville.

The other train piece, "Dixie Flyer Blues," came into final form in the mid-1920s at a summer resort at, of all places, Idlewild, Michigan. DeFord had gone there on his vacation with his landlord, Mr. Will Sarden, whose sister owned the resort. He had stayed there about a month, visiting such places as Grand Rapids and St. Joseph; one day, while sitting in his room, he saw a black cat get up in his window, and he said to himself, "I'm going to make me up a blues song." He got out his harp and worked out a new train song, one "altogether different" from "Pan American."

I play the "Pan American" song just like the natural train itself. . . . It's just straight out, just like a train. Natural whistle. Natural sound.

The "Dixie Flyer," it's got the sound of pumping, but it don't pump as long and it's short pumping, and blow the whistle different. Make the difference in the whistle. The "Pan American," it's got the whistle right. You can hear the railing pop every once in a while, while it's rolling. When it "cha, cha, cha, cha," like that.

DeFord was somewhat partial to the Dixie Flyer, which he called "a slick train" with "a pretty brass bell":

That train didn't stop at small places like Newsom's Station. They'd slow down just a little a couple of miles before the station and they'd start blowing and ringing that bell. They had good brass back then and that bell, it was the prettiest thing you ever seen. Shiny. When that train came through, that bell'd be ringing.

I can see it now. It was running so fast, the smoke would be laying down, jumping out of the stack and curling around on top of the coaches. When they'd see that track was clear, they'd shift into the last gear and throw that throttle wide open. That done me more good than scratching my head.

It was the "Pan American," though, that became the favorite of the Opry staff and the audience. In fact, it became almost an Opry theme song in the show's early years; every night brought requests to play it, and DeFord usually obliged. Though both the Pan American and Dixie Flyer were steam-powered locomotives, DeFord later began to add a diesel whistle in his renditions. "I rode a diesel engine train to Chicago a few times, but I didn't care for it," he recalled. "I did like that whistle, though, so I put it on my train." In one of DeFord's earliest and most famous publicity photos for the Opry, he is shown standing in front of the WSM microphones, with a megaphone attached to his harp, and near his right hand a wire rack with wooden and metal pieces which he could hit with a stick as he performed, adding sound effects for his train pieces.

The "Pan American" had two other symbolic roles in the early Opry history. In late 1927, it was DeFord's playing. of this tune that inspired George Hay to name the radio show "The Grand Ole Opry" (see Chapter 5). And in the mid-1930s WSM found that its transmitter tower was located right beside the L&N line as it ran south through the suburb of Brentwood. Some engineer came up with the idea of placing an open mike by the track to catch the Pan American as it left Nashville, headed for New Orleans. "The Pan" would blow its whistle, and the sound would go out over WSM, every day, like clockwork. The feature became one of the most popular on the station in the 1930s and formed a real-life counterpart to the favorite piece by the station's favorite harmonica soloist.

Even on a show that featured good harmonica players like Herman Crook and Dr. Humphrey Bate, DeFord stood out as a unique stylist. This is obvious when one compares his vintage records with those of other Opry harp players. Like most traditional musicians, he was unable to define exactly what he did in technical terms, but in later years he did explain why he thought his style was so different. He noted that he could play like other musicians, but not often, and then only to demonstrate how his style differed from theirs: "My timing is different from theirs. I play double. I got a double sound. I can't play single. It doesn't sound good to me." Some of the Opry performers used to question him about his style of playing, wanting to know how he made certain sounds, or certain combinations, or how he could keep rhythm going while he played melody lines (like a Merle Travis-style guitar solo). He could never answer this to their satisfaction. Laughing, he recalled one particular incident: "Dr. Bate had me open my mouth one time to see why I played like I do. All he found was some old, crooked teeth."

He liked to claim that no one could really understand his music, or his style:

You can't x-ray it or do blueprints like a doctor or engineer to understand it. It's just in me. I can't help it. I don't ask nobody to help me or show me how to do it. I just do it.

You hear something all the time with my music. Other people's music is good, but it's missing something, I think. I add time to vacant space.

DeFord explained this by showing the space between his fingers. Other harmonica players just played the dominant notes, as indicated by his fingers; when he played, he filled in the spaces with minor notes as well. He made his harmonica "talk."

A harp ought to talk just like you and me. All the time I'm playing, I'm talking, but most people don't understand it. In blowing a harp, it's just like going to school to learn foreign languages. You got to learn how to make it talk in all sorts of ways. I can make it say whatever I want to.

He was especially proud at how "clear" his notes were when he did this; "That's where I lose 'em at," he said, referring to other harp players.

DeFord's music was different from that of other Opry stars in another important way. When most of the Opry's musical technicians, like Sam McGee or Arthur Smith, finally worked out a piece to their satisfaction, they tended to "freeze" the arrangement and use it over and over again, playing it the same way each time. DeFord continually altered his work, revising it in subtle ways. He explained:

Most people play in one gear—up and down. That's like driving all the way to Franklin [about thirteen miles from Nashville] in first gear. I'll be blowing one minute in one gear and the next minute in another gear.

Nobody will ever catch up with my music because I don't stay nowhere long with my music. I change. It's like sickness. It changes from a cold to pneumonia, and if not cured, goes to TB, and you may be long gone—but anyway, it changes. It don't stay the same.

He had an amazing array of what he called "notes and licks," which he used in an endless variety of ways. For example, he liked to "sweeten up" a piece by hitting a high note and then immediately dropping the next one a full octave or more. Other times he would "throw a little judo" in his music by putting in an unexpected lick of some sort (as in his 1928 recording of "John Henry"). His fondness for "sounds" rather than individual notes meant that he was ceaselessly experimenting with various unorthodox chords or what fiddlers would call "double stops." He was also a master of dynamics, swooping in one phrase from a loud, braying trainlike phrase to a gentle, fluttering arpeggio. The result was a style that was uniquely his—neither entirely the harsh sound of the blues harp nor the mellow sweet sound of old-time country music. And it was about to make DeFord the most famous harp player in the nation.

8

"We Got Their Best Harp Player"

By 1928, DeFord had settled into a weekly routine on the Opry, often opening the program on Saturday nights at 8:30 and then doing a second segment at 10:30 or 11:00. He was appearing every single week, twice as often as any other performer, and establishing himself as one of the show's most popular acts. In the fall of that year, however, events conspired to change all this, and to threaten the entire direction of DeFord's career. The unlikely catalyst for these events was the annual football game between Vanderbilt University (in Nashville) and the University of Tennessee (in Knoxville). This annual state rivalry customarily concludes the football season for both teams, and in 1928 the competition was even keener than usual. For the previous twelve years, Tennessee had been unable to beat Vanderbilt, but so far in the 1928 season the Tennessee Volunteers had won all seven of the games they had played, and many Knoxville fans felt this would be their year. More than five thousand of them made the nearly 200 mile trip from Knoxville to Nashville, where they joined some 20,000 Vanderbilt fans at Dudley Field on a bright November 17 Saturday afternoon.

One of those who came from Knoxville for the game was W. C. Taylor, manager of the Pay Cash Grocery Company on Depot Avenue in downtown Knoxville. He was an emcee on Knoxville's fledgling radio station WNOX, owned by Sterchi Brothers Furniture Company and located in the St. James Hotel. The station managed to mount two-hour programs on Tuesdays, Thursdays, and Saturdays; Taylor was known to radio audiences as "Pay Cash" Taylor for his work on the Saturday-night musical variety show. Knowing even this early that radio was a good way to advertise, he came to Nashville with two purposes in mind: to see

Tennessee beat Vanderbilt, and to lure DeFord Bailey back to Knoxville as a drawing card for his radio show. He was successful on both counts: Tennessee won the game 6 to 0 in a hard-fought contest, and DeFord Bailey agreed to leave Nashville for Knoxville. "We not only beat their football team, but we got their best harp player too," Taylor boasted later.

Taylor was impressed not only by DeFord's talent but also by his appearance. He later told the harmonica player that he never would have hired him if he had "been dressed in a rattlesnake stripe suit, 'cause I would have known I couldn't do anything with you." As it was, he had no reservations when he met DeFord. "I had on a smooth, navy-blue dark suit," DeFord recalled. "Them kind of clothes will stand anywhere."

For his part, DeFord was ready to talk business. He was less than happy with the kind of money he had been getting at WSM, and with George Hay's attitude toward it. Though it is not widely known, DeFord was paid "something" for every appearance he ever made on radio, even from the earliest days. "Dad [Pop Exum of WDAD] gave me a couple of dollars every time I played on his show," he said. "Judge Hay paid me two dollars at first, then increased it to seven dollars a night." DeFord was probably unique in this regard; there is no record of any other performer on the Opry this early being paid anything for their work on the show. And, when payments began, they were in the neighborhood of five dollars. These earliest payments Hay probably made out of his own pocket; the later ones came from the station. In addition, when DeFord first began on the air, several admiring fans sent him money in fan mail. The Opry management found out about this, though, and at once put a stop to it. DeFord said they announced over the air "not to send any money, coin or check, to any of the performers." From then on, someone at the station looked at all his mail before it was forwarded to him, an action that seriously bothered him. The public, he felt, "would have made me wealthy if WSM would have let me get my money right. It was terrible. Looking back on it, I guess I was just a civilized slave, as far as money was concerned."

The paternalistic manner in which Hay and WSM handled his finances added to his concern. As noted above, when DeFord made his Brunswick recordings in New York, Hay took a commission of 25 percent of his $400 payment for recording. The remaining $300 was also sent to Hay, who gave DeFord a lump sum payment of $75 and then doled out the balance to him each Saturday night in $10 cash payments. As if this were not enough, the $10 replaced DeFord's normal $7 nightly fee; where he should have rightfully gotten $17 a night under this installment system, he received only $10. Once the balance of the $300 was exhausted, DeFord went back to his regular pay of $7 a night. "I wasn't getting nowhere at WSM," he said in retrospect. Thus when "Pay Cash" Taylor came over and offered DeFord $20 a night to appear in Knoxville—almost three times his Opry wage—he was ready to go. He agreed to move to Knoxville at once, and was making plans to settle down there permanently. He went so far as to tell his relatives that, when he came back to Nashville, "it would be in a box."

Taylor wanted DeFord to leave with him that Saturday evening, but there was a matter of giving the Opry at least two weeks' notice. An arrangement was finally worked out, amidst Hay's anger and concern, to have DeFord commute for a couple of weeks, staying in Knoxville but returning Saturday nights for the Opry. His first WNOX appearance was set for Wednesday, November 21, just four days after the football game. The *Knoxville Journal* carried a special announcement about the program, noting that it would feature DeFord Bailey and that it would run from 8:00 to 10:00 P.M.

The initial program was more of a success than even Taylor expected. In a scene reminiscent of Uncle Jimmy Thompson's first appearance on WSM, DeFord's show ran far past the scheduled time, ending at midnight rather than ten o'clock. The radio column in the next day's edition of the *Knoxville News-Sentinel* reviewed the show, explaining just what happened:

> When it comes to playing the French harp (they say the correct name is harmonica, but we don't call it that here), DeFord Bailey stands out as one of those who can make the instrument talk and trill.
>
> I had heard him play once or twice on WSM, but had not given his playing much attention until he played last night over WNOX. The harp has its note limitations, as we all know, and that's one thing that makes Bailey's playing more remarkable. He actually brings out half notes when there aren't any such notes on the instrument. Of course, the most difficult thing, which is more a stunt than music, is the locomotive trill, which he puts into his blues selections.
>
> Telegrams for request numbers over WNOX last night made the station seem like a fifty-kilowatt station, instead of its rated power of one kilowatt. There were at least fifty long distance phone calls and over a hundred telegrams, and it was nothing for the northern and southern borders of the U.S. to report the station "coming in like a local." W. C. Taylor, of the Pay Cash Grocery Company, must have given away a hundred boxes of chewing gum.

He offered one to each of those who sent messages. WNOX stayed on the air until about midnight.

As the format for the show gradually jelled, listeners were encouraged to send in requests every week, and many did: telegrams came from all over East Tennessee as well as from Kentucky, North Carolina, and Virginia. The show was broadcast live from the St. James Hotel every Wednesday night. Originally it was called *The Pay Cash Show*, but as other sponsors came on board—notably JFG Coffee, then as now a regional favorite—the name was changed to the *Big Four Variety Program*. It was scheduled as a two-hour show, then expanded to a three-hour show, and often ran longer than that. DeFord shared the show with two other regular acts: a singing group called the Pay Cash Warblers and later the Big Four Quartet, and a stringband called Cal & His Gang. "Cal" was Cal Davenport, a banjo player who worked at a local factory, and whose brother Hubert was generally considered to be the best local harmonica player before DeFord came on the scene. The band made several recordings for Vocalion in Knoxville in 1929, and throughout the 1930s played and toured for JFG Coffee and for the colorful promoter Cas Walker. Davenport's stringband sounded something like that of DeFord's old Opry friend Dr. Humphrey Bate.

Shortly after DeFord arrived in Knoxville, Taylor found him a room in a boardinghouse on East Vine Street; the landlords were Mr. and Mrs. Goodman, a middle-aged Black couple. DeFord came to like the Goodmans and stayed with them the entire time he was in Knoxville. "They was nice people. It was just like home. Couldn't tell no difference. I had a nice front room with a piano. I'd play on that piano when I got lonesome, and sing." DeFord also liked Knoxville. Vine Street was home to a number of Blacks in the city (in fact, one of the local Black stringbands, headed by fiddler Howard Armstrong, celebrated it with a 1930 Vocalion record called "Vine Street Rag"); DeFord felt free to go wherever he wanted, though, usually on foot. Reflecting back on these days, he said that in Knoxville, unlike some other southern cities, Black and white people always got along well. Certainly he felt comfortable in the city. One of the first things Taylor had done was to introduce Bailey to the local police and assure them that he was "okay," and this added to his feeling of "being at home" in the town.

After a couple of months in Knoxville, though, DeFord became restless and began thinking about moving on. He was almost thirty years old and at the peak of his abilities; his fan mail was proving to him that he could appeal to fans all over the country, not just in the South. His popularity with sponsors was showing him that he could sell a lot of products just by performing on their radio shows. His long-time ambition to be a successful, full-time musician was compelling him to make a break for the big time. Among his new local friends was a well-off Jewish man who wanted DeFord to go with him in his new Cadillac to California and try his luck out there. Bailey was sorely tempted and had just about decided to make the trip when Taylor intervened.

Taylor, it turned out, had made a promise to Judge Hay, before DeFord left Nashville, to take care of the musician, and he was wary of the California trip. He felt that, if he was going to lose DeFord, it should be to Nashville rather than California. Bringing all this to a head in February 1929, Taylor came to DeFord and told him that he would buy his train ticket to Nashville and would take him to the train; if DeFord refused, he would have to drive him back to Nashville himself. He said, "I promised Hay I'd bring you back [there] if you ever left me."

Faced with this kind of ultimatum, DeFord agreed and, in the third week of February, took the train for Nashville. When he arrived in town, he went straight to George Hay's office and, as per arrangement, had him telephone Taylor back in Knoxville to confirm that he had arrived. After several days of negotiation, Hay was able to talk him out of the California idea and convince him to stay at WSM. DeFord insisted, though, that the days of $7 shows were over; he wanted at least the $20 a show he was getting in Knoxville. If a small, developing station like WNOX could afford it, then surely a major powerhouse like WSM could as well. Reluctantly, Hay agreed, and DeFord made his return to the Opry on February 23, 1929.

For a time, he assumed the role of a dapper man about town. At the peak of his abilities, he was making good money and getting a national reputation as a radio and record star. He had more money than he needed for his upkeep, and his foster brother and sisters were now out on their own; much of his extra money went into clothes. "I wore the very best there was in those days," he recalled. Demonstrating this, a 1929 photo, a formal portrait by prominent Nashville photographer J. Frank West, shows DeFord in his Sunday best. His $25 suit had been bought in Knoxville; his $25 overcoat was from T. A. Bowman's; his $20 top hat came from Petway Revis; the shoes were $12.50 Florsheims; the white scarf was worth $3, and the walking stick was worth $3.50. And these were 1929 prices, when hamburger was 15 cents a pound. In his own words, DeFord was a "sharp dude."

Clark Odum, DeFord's foster father, had died in Detroit in 1928, and by now DeFord had rented a room in the home of Mr. and Mrs. William Sarden, on

Tremont Street. Nearby, on Fourteenth Avenue South, lived the Sardens' attractive teenage niece, Ida Lee Jones. She loved music and loved to dance; she would often come over to the Sardens' to hear DeFord practice and to dance while he played. Soon the two were dating, and in 1929 they decided to get married. By now DeFord was convinced he could make a living as a musician and was willing to take on the responsibility of a wife and family. In doing so, he effectively gave up much serious hope of moving on to California or out of Nashville; if he did entertain it, the events of October 1929 put an even more definite end to it. With Black Friday came the Great Depression, and before long WSM announced that they were cutting the salary of all performers and staff exactly in half. "Half a loaf was better than no loaf at all," DeFord remembered. It must have been with some pride that, when DeFord and Ida Lee had their first child, DeFord Junior, on January 3, 1932, at Nashville General Hospital, DeFord was able to list his occupation on the birth certificate as "Musician."

Two daughters followed: Dezoral Lee, on October 15, 1934, and Christine Lamb, on December 29, 1936. The latter was named after Christine Lamb, a white self-styled "blues singer" who was a regular on WSM's pop music shows, and who, like DeFord, had performed on WDAD. If Christine had been a son, DeFord recalled, the plan was to name him after Harry Stone, the Opry announcer. Such plans show just how great a role DeFord saw WSM and the Opry playing in his life during this time.

The children grew up hearing their father on the Opry and were soon showing that they had inherited some of his musical skills. When Dezoral was barely nine months old, for instance, DeFord sat her on his lap and handed her his harp—upside down. She played on it that way for a moment, then quietly turned it right side up and continued to play. DeFord was delighted. "Dezoral learned to play the harp pretty good as a child," he later recalled. The other children took up other instruments but preferred "to leave the harp playing to daddy." On occasion, Ida Lee would bring the small children to the Opry to watch their father; they would normally sit quietly at the rear of the auditorium, or the Dixie Tabernacle, where the show moved in the mid-1930s. DeFord remembered once coming out on stage and hearing his daughter Christine call out, "Momma, there's Daddy blowing his harp!" "My wife told the child to hush," he remembered, "but the white people sitting nearby laughed and said, 'Let her talk out.'"

As his family grew and the Depression lengthened, DeFord found himself looking for other ways to supplement his Opry income. About 1930 he opened a barbeque stand on a vacant lot next to his house at 130 Lafayette Street, a road

*Bailey's children. Left to right, Dezoral, Christine, and DeFord Jr.
Photograph given to Morton by Bailey for use in biography.*

that was also the Murfreesboro Pike, a main route into Nashville. DeFord built the stand himself out of cedar wood, designing it to resemble a log cabin. A late-1930s WSM News Service publicity piece stated that the harmonica player "in his spare time" cooks "Southern-styled dishes and entertains customers at his 'Grand Ole Opry-DeFord Bailey Barbeque Stand.'" DeFord had hired "a first class cook" named George, "a real barbeque man"; between the two of them, they kept the stand going night and day for eight years.

He also became a landlord, routinely renting out rooms in his house. As he moved in and around the Edgehill neighborhood, living on streets like Thirteenth and Fifteenth Avenue South, Tremont, Brinkley, and Lafayette, he deliberately sought out houses larger than he and his family needed, with the idea of renting out spare rooms. In an age of segregated hotels and housing, there was almost

DeFord Bailey's home at 130 Lafayette Street in Nashville, where he rented out rooms. Photo courtesy of the Metropolitan Development and Housing Agency.

always a need for rooms to rent. On Lafayette, he went so far as to rent out rooms by the week and even by the night, like a motel. He put a sign in his window advertising rooms for rent; soon he was doing a comfortable sideline business in this as well. He did so well, in fact, that one Nashville official tried to get him to register as a hotel.

> They come out there, one white fellow did, with a big book, you know, wanted me to sign some papers and I wouldn't sign them. I said, "What's it for?" "Well, you got a hotel here and you got to have a little license." He didn't think I had no sense. I carried it uptown to WSM, to their lawyer.

"If you'd signed that thing, why you'd been paying as much as the Andrew Jackson [Nashville's largest and finest hotel]," he told me.

I wouldn't sign 'em. I said, "I ain't got 15 cents worth of nothing in there." It was right cute. I laughed about it. He just argued and argued. Why, you know, you got people here and you got a good location . . . blah, blah, blah. I ain't never paid no license for nothing.

To get around town and do all the chores these extra businesses demanded, DeFord used a bicycle, and this soon became another part of his legend. He had learned to ride when living in Franklin, when he was fifteen; he never owned a car, and everywhere he went, he went on his bike. He rode it to visit relatives, to go shopping, to go to work, and to even take his kids to school. (He would have Junior in a special seat behind him, holding on to Christine, the youngest, while Dezoral held on to her father.) He also would take his bike onto the Opry stage, and do tricks as part of his act. Nor did he hesitate about long distances: when he was young he would routinely ride the hilly roads to Franklin and back, a round trip of twenty-six miles.

He continued to ride his "wheel," as he called it, until his early forties. Over the years, he naturally became quite skilled at riding and doing various tricks on it. For example, he could be riding along and lean down to pick a dime off the ground without stopping his bike. He could also ride long distances down a narrow railway track without falling off. He had one special bike, a Connell Racer, that he kept for sixteen years; it was this one that he rode down to the Opry every Saturday night, bringing it inside the door during the show and riding home on it afterwards late at night. Listeners knew about his bike as well; a 1936 cartoon sent in by a fan showed a tiny DeFord blowing his harp while riding his "wheel." "Nearly everybody in Nashville knowed that bicycle," he explained. "Police knowed it. I took that thing everywhere."

He had the bicycle fixed up with lights, reflectors, and other special features that "didn't come with it from the factory." Some of these features were innovative for the 1930s.

I had everything on it. I had a speedometer on it and all kinds of whistles. Had it all. That's the way I got in the radio business. . . . He [Pop Exum of WDAD] had a store, an automobile store, where you buy all kinds of lights to put on your car, you know. Well, I bought them things and put 'em on the side of my wheel, and put one on the fender and on the front wheel and in back, and that style finally came out from the factory.

I had a Buick light that you put on top of the fender for a parking light. Well, I put that on top of my fender and bored a hole down through there and had a battery running all up in there, and taped up in there, and put it back there for it to hang. I'd turn my button on and off. . . .

After then, they [the manufacturers] put lights back there . . . . They noticed me and how I had my wheel decorated.

Why, I'd come down through a street with my headlight on my fender. It was pretty. V-shaped. . . . And I had a stop light. I had a button I mashed when I was getting ready to stop. It come on. I had another that turned green and turned yellow. It turned orange color first. Then it changed to that other color and then come green to go. . . . I had a stop light, a go light, and everything.

With such devices, DeFord felt safe riding his bicycle at night. He knew he could be seen by anyone else on the road; his reflectors, or "flashbacks" as he called them, were in his wheel spokes and turned over as he pedaled. "Cars would flash on it and my wheel would look like it was on fire. First one color, then another one. Red, green, blue. I was something else. That thing was pretty at night time. Cars would be coming, and that wheel would just shine." It was only when he thought it was hurting his health that DeFord stopped riding his wheel: "I put it down just all at once. I got on my bicycle up there on Twelfth Avenue and I coasted from Twelfth to Stevens Street. And when I got off, my heart just went, 'Bup, bup, bup.' I said, if I can't sit down and coast down the hill, I ain't got no business trying to ride up a hill. So I pushed the thing home that night and I ain't had no bicycle since. Sold it. To be sure I got rid of it, I sold it to the junk man."

All in all, the 1930s were a good time for DeFord. He was enjoying life as a family man, making a good living from his performing and his other enterprises, and was a well-known figure around Nashville. There were worse ways to weather the Depression. But his salary at the radio station itself was still not enough to live on, and even with his other income, he still found it necessary to do what almost all the other early country musicians did to make any real money: go out on personal-appearance tours. These tours were to become at once the source of some of his greatest triumphs—and greatest trials.

9

"Had Some Good
Times Together"

In early 1933, WSM organized their Artists' Service Bureau, essentially a booking agency designed to promote personal appearances for the WSM stars, both popular and country. It would set up tours for artists, help with publicity, and allow the artist to advertise the tour on the air—all for a commission. In theory, this allowed the performers to get out on show dates and make better money than the station could afford to pay them in weekly wages, thus allowing the performers to keep at the music on a full-time basis. WSM was by no means unique in this regard; dozens of stations around the country were experimenting with similar systems. By now DeFord was one of the most popular members of the Grand Ole Opry cast. "Uncle Dave [Macon] was the Opry's favorite performer, and I was the second," he remembered. Acuff himself, who came to show in 1938, recalls that Bailey in those days "could draw a crowd when no one knew Roy Acuff." Kirk McGee, who often traveled with Uncle Dave and often worked with DeFord, said, "I never saw DeFord fail. He would knock them out!" Vito Pellettieri, the longtime stage manager of the show, said, "DeFord was loved all over the South." This popularity, coupled with DeFord not being part of any larger organized group, won him dozens of offers to go out on the road with various groups. These trips augmented his income, added to his popularity, and left him with a wealth of memories—some pleasant, some bitter.

Shortly after he joined the Opry, DeFord turned down his first offer to travel with some of the WSM staff, including George Hay and Harry Stone, who were going to Texas to help start up a new radio station. (Later Stone and Hay went back a time or two because "WSM was behind the new station.") Soon afterwards, though, he began to accept offers from people who organized tours and, after the Artists' Service Bureau was formed, from the promoters in that office. It didn't take him long to realize that he wasn't being paid in accordance with his drawing power or even on an equitable basis with other members of the tours. At first, what he got depended on the success of the tour; it was seldom over $5 a day, and often far less. Before long, Judge Hay stepped in and decreed that, regardless of the size of the gate, and regardless of who traveled with him, DeFord would get a fixed flat rate of $5 a day. Some groups stopped using him after that, but it at least assured Bailey of a minimum wage.

On one occasion, an Opry star would defraud DeFord by pretending that the band had been paid in whiskey and offer DeFord his "share" in the form of one or two bottles; he knew DeFord was a teetotaler and would refuse the bottles. It was only after two friends, the Delmore Brothers, told DeFord that the whole story about the whiskey pay was a sham that he caught on and stopped working with the man.

Though Hay's initial intent in the decree was well motivated and in DeFord's best interests, later on the harmonica player began to suffer because of the "flat fee" rule. Alton Delmore remembered one particular date where, had DeFord been on percentage of the gate like everyone else, he would have netted $39 instead of his flat fee of $5; to their credit, they paid him the $39. There was also the problem that DeFord could not always control his expenses on the road, which had to come out of the $5 a day. The result was that he seldom came home with more than $10 for a full week's work on the road. "Sometimes I was sleeping in cars trying to get home with something," he recalled. "It was pitiful."

Through the 1930s, DeFord toured regularly, playing with other Opry favorites at tent shows, state and county fairs, auditoriums, schoolhouses, and theaters around the country. He traveled thousands of miles and performed in hundreds of cities, always going by car, on narrow state highways, always having to get back to Nashville on Saturday night to make the broadcast. There were so many trips that DeFord, fifty years later, found it difficult to distinguish one from the other. He traveled with virtually all of the show's regulars at this time, including Uncle Dave Macon, Alton and Rabon Delmore, Arthur Smith, Sam and Kirk McGee, Sarie & Sallie, Lasses White & Honey Wilds, Paul Warmack & the Gully Jumpers, the Fruit Jar Drinkers, Curt Poulton & the Vagabonds, Clayton McMichen, Ken Hackley, and, later, Roy Acuff and Bill Monroe. Only a few of the trips, and some of the incidents, stood out vividly in his memory.

This is understandable since most of the groups would be gone all week performing in several different towns. They often drove all day to make a show in another town night after night. Sometimes they would leave Nashville on Saturday night after the Opry show on their way to one of numerous cities in the Carolinas, Ohio, Virginia, or even farther away. After a week on the road, they always tried to be back in Nashville for the Saturday-night show. While they usually got in late Friday night, sometimes they wouldn't make it until just before the show on Saturday. Fiddlin' Sid Harkreader says that he and DeFord, along with Mrs. Edna Wilson and Mrs. Margaret Waters, better known as comedians "Sarie & Sallie," made several tours through East Tennessee, West Virginia, North and South Carolina in the 1930s. DeFord remembered going with them but didn't remember the details of any of those trips. He did remember one trip to Pennsylvania with Sarie & Sallie and Sam and Kirk McGee:

> A bunch of us left here one evening and went to Lebanon, Pennsylvania. Sarie & Sallie, and I believe Mr. Kirk and Mr. Sam, too.
>
> They [Sarie & Sallie] wore bonnets and them long dresses, ruffles, big legged underwear. Come out on the stage with them things and pull up their dress. People would laugh. They was a sight. They talked funny. Like Minnie Pearl. Was comedians. I believe they sang, too. I went with them a lot of places.

He remembered making several trips with Judge Hay. On one of them they took the Greyhound bus to Little Rock; they later made two trips to Cincinnati, and several to towns in Kentucky and Tennessee. They went on one trip to South Carolina to play on a radio show that Ed McConnell had. "McConnell was a good piano player," DeFord said, "who had played on WSM." DeFord played for a group of railroad safety men in the 1920s on a train trip from Nashville to Columbia and back. Especially eager to hear him play his "train," they had him play it "over and over," Bailey remembered. The longest trip DeFord recalled was the time the group went to Franklin, Louisiana, and then to Asheville, North Carolina. This was a trip of thirteen hundred miles. They stopped off in Nashville just long enough to play on the Opry.

One of the most unusual groups he participated in was composed of himself, Curt Poulton's wife, and two other white women. The four of them traveled together for three or four months. They worked out of St. Louis, Missouri, during the week but returned to Nashville each weekend. When they first started out, one of the Opry's top officials told DeFord "to stick with" the three women. He took the responsibility quite seriously. As a Black man, he felt honored being invited to tour with three white women. He did his best to make sure that nothing happened to them. He acted much like a bodyguard, keeping his pistol handy. "When I told Mr. Craig I'd stick with them, I took that like an oath. I had my gun and I wouldn't bother nobody, but if somebody had put a hand on them and hit them or something, it would've been too bad for him and me, too. I was their protection."

He seldom went by himself to any other city for a performance. On one occasion, however, he did take a train trip on his own to Macon, Georgia. Comedian Honey Wilds and other WSM artists were playing there, and they had wired for him to come down to join them. The theater management had expected him to perform and was upset that he wasn't with Wilds and his group.

The shows they gave around the country were quite popular. Adults who came to the shows usually paid 50 cents apiece, with children paying less. Even though times were hard during the Depression, scores of people were willing to pay to see the performers in person. People had come to love the musicians they had heard on the Saturday-night Opry. Most of the shows lasted one hour; in each one, DeFord played two or three tunes. "You don't ever give them all they want, or they'll lose interest in you," he said shrewdly. "This way, they never got tired of me."

Before the advent of adjustable microphones, DeFord often had to stand on something, usually a Coca-Cola crate, in order to reach the microphone. As an alternative to a microphone or other form of public address system, he generally carried a megaphone, which he had designed himself, to attach to his harp. When he played, DeFord usually held his harp with only one hand. He made it look as if it required no effort at all. He didn't jerk his hand back and forth, but moved his wrist in a smooth, rhythmical manner. His advice to other would-be harmonica players was to "hold a harp like I do and then move your hand like power steering on a car, not like standard steering. It's important," he said, "to move your hand smooth." Asked what key he most often used, DeFord answered:

> I use G and A and B. If I was going to play for some big money, like making a record, I'd either use an A or a G, one of the two. See, they got a good tone and good bass and you can choke it down any way you want to . . . and it'll sound natural and it's firm and clear and everything.
>
> And a B, it's kind of mellow and soft, but it's not as tough as A and G. And C is good, but it's too fine to work by yourself. That's good for the piano. That's a very fine harp. To tell you the truth, you might say it could be the best harp, but it's not the best harp for me, played by yourself.

Bailey with his foot on a Coca-Cola crate.
Photograph given to Morton by Bailey for use in biography.

On tour, DeFord usually played only his harmonica; however, when he was with Roy Acuff & the Smoky Mountain Boys, he would sometimes play one of their guitars or banjos in his left-handed, upside-down style. Often he would sing along. "It was a novelty to see him play," Kirk McGee said, "since the guitar was almost as big as he was." Seeing and hearing him play "I'm Going to Kansas City" on the guitar always pleased the crowds.

As with the harp, DeFord made "double notes" on the guitar. This was quite intentional: "I want the same movement playing my guitar with my fingers as I do playing my harp with my mouth." Like his harp, his guitar had to "talk in all kinds of languages—German, French, Italian, and more." Like most Black performers, he "picked" a guitar with his fingers. He didn't strum the instrument or use a pick.

> I never will forget. Mr. Arthur Smith said, "I don't mean anything by this, DeFord, but you play just like a nigger."
>
> We got a blues sound. A Black man picks with his finger. Most white men would strum. You can strum, humm, humm. You got a tune, but you ain't doing nothing.
>
> They pick a banjo, but . . . some of them would pick it with a picker. It was easy. But that don't sound right.

He used all five fingers on his left hand to pick the strings while his thumb and index finger did the work on the neck of the guitar (where he put small black dots to guide him). By adjusting the bridge, he set the guitar strings down low, close to the guitar. He usually played in the key of E. In playing a six-string guitar, the left-handed DeFord turned the instrument upside down with the bass string on the bottom. Unlike most left-handed musicians, he did not restring the guitar. DeFord knew only one other left-handed performer, Robert Lunn, who played this way. "He played the guitar with strings the same way I do and tuned the same," DeFord said, "but he couldn't do like I do."

DeFord learned to play that way when he was growing up and was using someone else's guitar. All of the guitar pickers he knew were right-handed, and he couldn't very well restring their guitars for his own occasional use; he had to play them as they were. Accordingly, he merely turned the guitar upside down and played it with his left hand. As time went on, he never thought of playing it any other way.

DeFord also played the banjo in the same upside-down manner, except with a faster stroke. "You have to play a faster time with a banjo than you do with a guitar," he acknowledged, adding that "there is a whole lot in the five strings on a banjo—anything you want to hear. The banjo is like talking. It can do anything your mind wants to do."

Perhaps it should also be pointed out that Bailey had played with a yo-yo on stage long before Roy Acuff ever came to WSM. In fact, the King of Country Music may have picked up the idea from him. DeFord was "pretty good" with a yo-yo, often carrying one with him when he went to the Opry and on tours. The crowds always liked it.

DeFord also experimented with various means of accompaniment to his music. He would sometimes precede "The Fox Chase" by blowing a horn like those used by hunters to call their dogs. Likewise, in playing "John Henry," he would occasionally add sound effects to simulate the clanking of metal as the legendary steel-driving man pounded feverishly away. At other times, he clacked sticks and bones together with one hand while holding his harp with the other. Once he cut a hole in the side of a toy airplane and put his harp in it. The airplane had a wheel on top of it, which could be pulled with a string. He would pull the string to turn it, and it would hum while he played the harmonica. "It sounded like an airplane," DeFord recalled, adding that he played it several times "on the air." According to "Bashful Brother Oswald," one of Roy Acuff's Smoky Mountain Boys, the performers normally gave three or four shows a day, sometimes as many as five or six. Theater management would often show a movie between their shows. Oswald says Bailey would sleep during the movie or sit in front of the audience and watch the movie. Other performers would go out, shoot pool, eat, have a drink or whatever—but not DeFord. While they were "out on the town," he spent most of those hours alone in the hotels or backstage.

Social norms of the period would have made socializing with his white associates difficult under any circumstances, but DeFord had little or no interest in such "good times" with them or anyone else, white or Black. He didn't drink and wasn't looking for companionship. If he had been so inclined, he could have found companions in the Black communities of most towns he went through. But he wasn't even tempted in that direction. As he put it, "There is always somebody smarter than you. You'll find yourself robbed or dead if you get too friendly. Need to keep to yourself. There is all kinds of people in the world. Treat all the same, but keep your distance."

Wherever he was, DeFord was always careful not to flash money around or talk to strangers. "I never showed no money," he claimed. When he toured, he always carried some change and small bills with him so he didn't have to pull out a big bill to pay for things he wanted: "I never pulled out a $10 bill to buy a newspaper or a cup of coffee. I kept up with the price and I always made sure I had the right change for it." He was especially careful in dealing with women: "The smartest things in the world are a woman and a panther. . . . A woman will outsmart you nearly every time. You don't have a chance. You remember John Dillinger. A woman got him. . . . A panther can think fast."

As a result, he usually remained behind where he would play on his harp or perhaps pick a little on someone's guitar. He often watched after the musical instruments and other valuables of the group. He didn't really like the responsibility of keeping up with the money box, but when he was asked to do so, he always agreed. "I was the safe man. . . . I didn't take nothing," he remembered. In traveling with one group, DeFord was asked to carry the receipts of all the shows in a handbag throughout the trip. Their reasoning was that no one would suspect his carrying their money.

It was about this time that DeFord began carrying a small Smith & Wesson pistol that he called "Old Bessie." He took it with him wherever he went, keeping it in his pants pocket where he could get to it easily. Soon, carrying the weapon became second nature to him; he thought little about it, "no more than carrying a toothpick." The Opry tour groups traveled through their share of rough backwoods country, and he felt he needed protection, not only from thieves but from "wild animals" he might encounter.

> I carried it [Old Bessie] for DeFord, for my protection. . . . I was more scared of animals than anything else. I always figured I could talk to a human being, but you can't talk to them wild animals and things. Back in them times, you didn't know what was gonna happen. I was out there on the road. . . . We'd see things just going to Louisville, bears and things. You could break down and could have an accident. Someone get killed and they'd smell blood and come around. If you got an old gun, you could shoot it. They can't stand that smoke and stuff. They're going somewhere. . . . Maybe by that time somebody else would come around. I had it for my protection.

DeFord's Opry colleagues knew about his pistol. Roy Acuff said he did not object because he knew "DeFord was not a violent man." The performers often kidded him about his gun. In fact, someone nearly always "reminded" him to bring his "artillery" with him when they started off on another trip. With DeFord looking after their equipment, none of the groups he was with ever lost any money or instruments. Some other groups from the Opry weren't so fortunate. According to DeFord, Sam McGee had his guitar stolen once when he was out on the road; someone took it out of its case and replaced it with an old beat-up one. McGee later found his guitar for sale in the Arcade in Nashville.

Another group left their money box on the side of the road while fixing a flat tire during the winter when the ground was covered with snow. This "happened in Virginia or somewhere up there," he said, "but some lady found it and called WSM in Nashville, so they got it back." Other things happened that weren't planned. They occasionally had car trouble; sometimes they got lost. One group with car problems also ran out of money; DeFord remembered they got home only by wiring WSM for money. He also remembered traveling through some rugged wilderness: "We drove a lot at night and went through some rough country with wild animals. I'd see something jump across the road in front of us with eyes as big as quarters. I'd know it was another cougar."

He never could forget one night in Ohio with Roy Acuff and his band. They crossed the Ohio River on a ferry. The operator told them there was a big panther on the side. They didn't think too much about it at the time, but when they stopped on the side of the road a few minutes later, they were all startled by an animal's loud piercing cry. "It sounded like it was right next to us. Mr. Roy said for all of us to get back in the car quick, because only little DeFord has got anything to protect himself with."

The roads were in bad shape back then. A group would often wear out a set of tires in a week. They didn't worry about it since the cars they drove were usually rented. DeFord said the rental cars cost $75 a week. If performers furnished their own cars, they got 7 cents a mile. Most of the automobiles "were good cars," always "four-door sedans," and "mostly . . . Chevrolets, Fords and Dodges. Mr. Bill Monroe, he liked Oldsmobiles. Oldsmobiles are extra good cars. Mr. Clayton McMichen had a Packard, a straight eight, the best they was back then." Usually there were five to six people in a group, all going in one car. A few groups, such as Ken Hackley, took two and even three carloads.

Not only the roads but sometimes the drivers were in bad shape. After a long week, they were usually worn out, sleepy, and tired. DeFord did not have a driver's license, and said he didn't know how to drive. Nevertheless, on a few trips with the Delmore Brothers, he tried to drive when they were way out in the country and "nobody else was fit to drive." On such occasions, he claimed he went only "about five miles an hour," but at least they "was moving." There were not many cars on the road in the middle of the night back then," he said. He never tried to pass another car. When he met one coming, he just stopped and waited for it to go by. Then he would start creeping along again. Since he could hardly see over the steering wheel, that was probably wise: "I set on a pillow, and still couldn't see. I looked straight out in front, way out yonder. I could stay in the road that way. You know, the car goes the way you look."

Most of the time Bailey sat behind the driver or in the front with him. In this way, he would help keep the driver awake. DeFord said that, while they were good drivers, they were all inclined to drive "too fast": "None of them walked along, but Bill Monroe was the fastest, though He would often drive at ninety or nine-ty-five miles an hour down country roads at night. I looked down on ninety-five many a time with Bill Monroe and him still mashing down on the gas—and it was raining. Once he ran off the shoulder of the road, and I got him to slow down a little for the rest of the trip."

On one occasion, the car DeFord was a passenger in sideswiped another car and hit a tree, but no one was hurt and it didn't amount to anything. Fortunately, none of the groups he traveled with ever had a serious accident. Most of the trips he made were enjoyable, but there were some exceptions. As he explained:

> Sam McGee saw me cry once. That was in Middlesboro, Kentucky, after I got cheated out of my money one time. We had played at a big theater in Evansville, Indiana. The owner's son told me that I was the only one he had seen to pack that theater, and they had made a whole lot of money. But the man in charge of our show had told me they lost money. Instead of $5, I got a dollar and a half. I got my hat and took a train home. They fired me for one month. Then later, Judge Hay called me to come down to see him and hired me back. He told me that they found out the man hadn't just cheated me out of my little $5, he had cheated them out of thousands of dollars, too.

DeFord suffered for years from one long trip he made in the middle of the winter. He rode all night from Nashville to Asheville, North Carolina, in freezing weather in a car that had been wrecked, with cold air coming in around one of the doors. He had to sit next to the bad door the entire trip; no one offered to swap places with him even for a few minutes. The continued exposure to the cold air for such a long period apparently damaged the nerves in his right shoulder and hip. Ever since then, he occasionally experienced considerable pain in those areas.

DeFord received a lot of joking and kidding from the performers he worked with, but it was all well intended and well received. "Everybody picked at him," Kirk McGee says. "It's a wonder he didn't get spoiled." One of those who "picked at him" the most was Robert Lunn, a left-handed guitar player with whom DeFord traveled extensively in the 1930s. Lunn enjoyed practical jokes and often tried them out on his fellow performers. Knowing that Bailey never smoked, if Lunn ever found DeFord dozing or sleeping, he delighted in putting a cigarette in Bailey's mouth. He would then wake him, kidding him about his newly acquired "habit." Characteristically, the good-natured DeFord took it all in stride. He enjoyed the humor even if it was at his own expense.

On stage, DeFord was occasionally a source of unexpected humor. When he was with Ken Hackley, he was pushed out on the stage in a big baby buggy and then got out of it and played his harp. This always "broke up the crowd," he said. Bailey saw the humorous side of his situation on the Opry and had no hesitation making jokes about himself: "I used to have them dying laughing. I'd get sleepy. Robert Lunn, you know, and me, we'd be setting in the back seat all the time. He'd fall on me and go to sleep, and I'd fall on him and go to sleep. I said, 'Just fall over here. I ain't going to fade on you, . . . I done faded.' I'd have more fun than a little bit with them."

He developed many friendships with Opry performers and staff that lasted for years. His relationships with all of those on the show were good, but he became especially close to some, including George Hay, the Delmore Brothers, and Uncle Dave Macon. DeFord "hit it off" with Judge Hay right from the beginning. Hay became not only his employer or "boss," but also his manager, his fan, and his friend. When Bailey wasn't traveling, he often worked for Hay cooking or doing odd jobs at Hay's home. It was only a short bicycle ride from Edgehill, where DeFord lived, to Hay's home in the university area of Nashville, and he enjoyed spending an occasional morning or afternoon helping the Judge at his home. DeFord usually "listened" to Judge Hay about most things and did whatever he asked him to do. However, there were a few things he wouldn't do even for the Judge. Wanting to create a hillbilly image for the Opry, Hay gave the various bands names like "the Possum Hunters," "the Fruit Jar Drinkers," and "the Dixie Clodhoppers." This went over so well that he decided to carry the theme further by having the performers wear overalls and other farm clothes when they appeared on the Opry and on tour. This was where DeFord drew the line. Like most of the other performers, he had always worn a coat and tie, and he, for one, did not want to change: "Me and overalls can't get along no kind of way, but I got me some back then. I wore them two times, then I went back to my coat and tie. Nobody said nothing to me. . . . They was just plain country and I was country enough to begin with."

As with most white-Black relationships in the South in the first half of this century, Judge Hay somewhat paternalistically "looked after" Bailey. For DeFord, an illiterate Black man, participation in the all-white cast in the 1920s and 1930s would have been extremely difficult, if not impossible, had he not had some white person to insure that he received fair treatment in dealing with white performers, theater owners, and others. Hay made certain that DeFord received his pay for his performances. Normally Hay even set the amount he received. Knowing "the way things was back then," DeFord took what he was given without objection.

And, all in all, DeFord believed that the Judge did "the best he could for me." Bailey thought of Hay as a friend. "We talked a lot," he remembered, although Hay talked very little with most of the performers. DeFord knew some of the difficulties that plagued the talented Judge. He knew Hay couldn't see well and wore special glasses. He also knew Hay was highly nervous and had other physical problems. "He got sick several times, would stay off two or three months." Hay was the regular announcer for the Opry. When he was not there, David Stone or his brother, Harry, would take Hay's place. As the years went by, they did more and more of the announcing. Hay officially retired in 1956 and died twelve years later on May 8, 1968, in Virginia Beach, Virginia.

DeFord believed the top management at National Life did not treat Hay properly in view of all he had done for them: "Like me, he got misused, too. He made that Grand Ole Opry. He brought it out to what it is today, but he wasn't treated the way he should've been. Me and him both got tricked in a way." DeFord was convinced that Hay's mental and physical condition made a difference in what ultimately happened to Bailey himself at the Opry. "If he'd been at himself like the rest of them, I'd have had something," DeFord claimed.

The relationship DeFord developed with Alton and Rabon Delmore, two guitar-picking brothers from Alabama, was different from that with Judge Hay. Like Hay, they "looked after" him, but theirs was more of a fraternal than a paternal relationship. Treating him much like a younger brother, they attempted to see that DeFord received the same treatment they did.

The Delmore Brothers, 1930s. Photograph given to Morton by Bailey for use in biography.

I went all over with the Delmores and sometimes with them and Uncle Dave. They had a Chevy, I think, and we went in it most of the time.

They come from Athens, Alabama, and one time we was playing down near there at Red Bay, and we went by their house. They treated me the same there as anywhere else. They was just good old boys.

They was the ones who told me I wasn't getting my money right all the time. They said most performers got some of their pay in whiskey. Since I didn't drink no alcohol, I didn't get no whiskey, and didn't get my money right.

The Delmores came to the Opry in 1933 as one of the show's first duet acts. They were there for about five years and became highly popular with the WSM radio audience. They had a close-harmony style, and most of their songs were original. Alton, quite a talented composer, wrote hundreds of tunes, including "Brown's Ferry Blues" and "Gonna Lay Down My Old Guitar."

DeFord liked to see and hear them perform. "They was good guitar pickers and they could sing, too." He particularly liked their style of music. Having grown up in a poor white North Alabama family, they were strongly influenced by much the same "country blues" that DeFord had heard as a child. Their music reflected that "they knew about the blues," he said. Another performer "who knew about the blues" was the legendary Uncle Dave Macon, banjo-picker and former mule-team driver. He had grown up hearing the same "country blues." DeFord met Uncle Dave soon after he started on the Opry. They shared experiences during numerous tours together:

> I slept in the room with him, rode with him, ate with him, held up his pants while he put them on. I'd talk with Uncle Dave about my problems.
>
> When he went in to eat, I'd tell him to get me a sandwich to eat; when he brought it to me, I'd say, "Thank you, Uncle Dave." He'd laugh and say, "Poor old Black man. I was aiming to charge him, but I can't charge him now. He's done thanked me for it." Then, he'd laugh, ha, ha, ha.

Like those thousands who paid to see their shows, DeFord himself always enjoyed seeing the "Dixie Dewdrop," as Uncle Dave was widely called. He had a wide repertoire of old-time tunes that included "Keep My Skillet Good and Greasy," "Chewing Gum," "Wreck of the Tennessee Gravy Train," "Never Make Love No More," "Bile Them Cabbage Down," "Give Me Back My Five Dollars," and "Country Ham and Red Gravy." Of all Uncle Dave's tunes, DeFord liked best "You Can't Do Wrong and Get By." He liked the message of the lyrics as well as the tune. "I don't care what you do wrong, it'll come back to you," he said. No matter what Uncle Dave played, he "always went over good" with his audiences, DeFord claimed. A veteran of vaudeville shows, he knew how to entertain a crowd and "never let them down."

Uncle Dave's success wasn't really due to his musical expertise. Although he was "good" on the banjo, DeFord said there were many others on the Opry who played as well or better. But none of them came close to Uncle Dave as an entertainer. His personality, his actions, and his style added elements described by DeFord as "the dressing," which made the difference and set him apart from other banjo pickers. As Bailey explained: "I seen a many a person who could beat Uncle Dave. I had some uncles who could beat him playing a banjo, but they didn't have what the old fellow said, 'the dressing' and the sweets and stuff to go with it like Uncle Dave. Uncle Dave had the pepper sauce and barbeque and everything else with his. He'd just sweeten his stuff up, if you know what I mean."

Other musicians would play "plain music," but not Uncle Dave, DeFord said. "He had so many things to go with it." DeFord pointed out that Uncle Dave always wore "a plug hat," a black Stetson with a rag around it. The hat "had a high crown and was turned up all around the edge." While he was performing, he would take the hat off with one hand, stand his banjo up with the other, and "hit them strings" with the rim of the hat. At the same time, he would be "noting with the fingers that was holding the banjo." And his music was only part of the show.

> He'd sing and holler and just cut up. . . . He was funny with it. . . . He was a comedian and a show. . . . Everybody loved to hear him and when the crowds clapped and cheered, he'd tell them, "I know I'm good." Then he'd laugh and everybody would just fall out.
>
> He had his [music] all sweetened up you know, and nobody else couldn't catch Uncle Dave, I don't care which a way they played. You wouldn't have nothing on him, no kind of way.

In DeFord's estimation, there were a few Opry performers whose musical talent was genuinely outstanding. Clayton McMichen, who led the Georgia Wildcats, was in this category. Earlier a member of Gid Tanner's Skillet Lickers, McMichen had made numerous recordings from 1926 to 1931. He left the Skillet Lickers in 1931 and set up his own group. DeFord said McMichen's fiddling was so stirring that it stimulated the other performers to reach new heights:

> Clayton McMichen had a good band. I worked with him for a long time. We went up to Chicago, Gary, and all kinds of places. . . .
>
> He was a little short man, like me. Had a round face. He was a real good fellow, too. I got my money from him. Whatever I wanted. It looked like he didn't care if we made any money or not. "We're all here together; we're going to eat," he'd say. Everybody was one; we was all together.
>
> He was a good fiddle player, maybe even a little better than Mr. Roy [Acuff]. He could draw that bow and make that fiddle talk. When he went before me, it'd raise my spirits and I'd make that harp talk. He'd stir us all. I'd get a spell on me and feel like really doing something.

During the 1920s and 1930s, the Opry had several other fine fiddlers, including George Wilkinson and Sid Harkreader. DeFord went out on tours with most of them, and he enjoyed being with all of them. One fiddler, however, made a special impression on him. This was Arthur Smith, who played for several years with Sam and Kirk McGee. They called themselves "the Dixieliners." Bailey recalled: "He played nearly every Saturday night for years. He was just a terrible good fiddler. I'd pay more attention to him than any of the others. It looked like all of his spirit was in the fiddle. He beat everything I've ever seen. It's like a preacher. You know, some of them can keep your attention, but some of them can move you. He could move you."

DeFord also traveled extensively with another fiddler, a young East Tennessean by the name of Roy Acuff. Roy brought his band of "Smoky Mountain Boys" to WSM in 1938. At that time Acuff was, as he acknowledged, an unknown person. In order to help publicize his group and draw a good crowd, he soon asked DeFord to accompany him and his band as they went out on tour. They traveled together for long periods of time during Acuff's first two or three years on the Opry. "I slept on his shoulder and he slept on mine," Acuff said. Wherever they went, DeFord was always a big drawing card for them. He never failed to bring out a crowd. Ultimately, Acuff would no doubt have been a success at WSM without Bailey, but his initial success there was expedited by his early association with such a longtime Opry favorite.

Much the same could be said of another well-known Opry performer, Bill Monroe, the Father of Bluegrass Music. He first came to WSM in October 1939 with his Blue Grass Boys. He quickly enlisted the "Harmonica Wizard" to go with him as he sought public exposure with the WSM listening audience. DeFord enjoyed his travels with Monroe:

I stayed with him for quite a while. We played in Kentucky, Virginia, and all kinds of places.

He was a good fellow to work with and a good musician. He'd treat you right. It didn't matter what I wanted to eat, he'd get it for me. He'd see I'd eat. What he promised to pay, you'd get it. He paid me seven dollars and a half a day, I think. He was as good a mandolin player as I ever heard. I think he played a Gibson mandolin.

Looking back over his travels and long association with so many outstanding musicians, DeFord acknowledged that he was fortunate to have had the opportunities that he did. Many country musicians of the period had been influenced by Black performers, and blackface comedy was common fare. DeFord, however, was the only African American in his day to perform regularly on an equal basis with white country performers before white audiences in Dixie and elsewhere.

10

"The Black and the White—
All Wanted to Hear the Same Tune"

Over the years, the Grand Ole Opry became identified as the music of the rural white South. With the exception of DeFord Bailey and, more recently, Charley Pride, it has had an all-white cast. The studio audiences, from the beginning, have been virtually "lily white" in composition. However, when the Opry first started, there was no attempt to limit the program to a white audience. In fact, some efforts were actually made to attract "a colored audience" as well. Bailey remembered that, in signing off one evening, Judge Hay said over the air that "colored people could come" to listen to Opry performances. "He let them know they was welcome." The Opry and all other WSM programs were designed to help National Life sell insurance. A large portion of National Life's business consisted of small policies popular with low-income customers, Black and white, in the South. Judge Hay told DeFord at one point that "half of National Life's money comes from colored people." He also said DeFord had helped make a lot of those sales.

DeFord was not the only Black performer on the early Opry. There were several Black singers who appeared at least a few times; DeFord said they were not able "to fit in" as successfully as he was. How did he manage to work with whites for years as the only Black on the Opry? "I just had plain old horse sense," was DeFord's standard response to the question. He usually followed his response with a discourse on dealing with people. "You'll live a long time if you know how to deal with people," he said, adding:

I've been studying people, two sets of people [Blacks and whites], since I was eleven years old. I remember setting on a fence watching the stock in the field. They didn't seem to notice no difference in the color of the other cows and horses. I wondered why it was different with people. That's when I first started trying to figure out people.

DeFord thought that, over the years, he had gained a "pretty good understanding" of people. Doubtless he had been in a position to gain valuable insight into the way people of both races view themselves and each other. He remembered that, when he was a child, his grandfather, who had been born a slave, warned him "to watch out for white folks with their fancy arithmetic." His grandfather often quoted an old saying among Blacks of that day: "figgers are figgers, oughts are oughts; all for the white man, none for the niggers." Yet DeFord was treated "like a son" by one white family—the Watsons—and in later years he came to know and care for a number of other white people with whom he worked.

It was his musical career, however, that put him in a truly unique position to "figure out" white people. He was the only African American to play regularly on any of the country music or old-time music radio shows that proliferated in the 1920s and 1930s, and one of the few in this period who could draw large crowds of white southerners. Most Black performers of the period performed primarily to Black audiences, but not DeFord Bailey. He played for both races, and his appeal was apparently even stronger in the white community than in the Black.

Accordingly, he was accepted into many white circles and activities. He participated in functions that few, if any, Blacks of his day would have dreamed of doing. The combination of his skills as a musician and his diminutive, non-threatening physical appearance opened doors for him that were not open to other Black people. He was exposed to things that few Blacks saw or experienced during the long years of Jim Crow.

On the surface, it would appear he was exempt from most of the indignities and humiliations for Blacks that are associated with the rigid segregation of the period. To some extent this was true. As he explained: "Jim Crow didn't mean a thing to me. When I got on the streetcar, I would go to the back, but most of the time someone would call me to come back up to the front and play a tune." On the other hand, he was probably more sensitive to and conscious of the rigid rules than were most Blacks of his day. He emphasized that he "stayed in his place" to avoid any possible problems: "I'd stay there with them [at the front of the streetcar], but if they got off before I did, I'd go back to my place on the streetcar. I didn't have to be told."

He had learned early what was appropriate. Once when he was at the state fair with Gus Watson and went off by himself for a few minutes, somebody came to send him out. Fortunately, Watson was able to persuade them otherwise. "No, he's not going out," DeFord remembered Watson saying. "He's with me." However, during the remainder of the time he was in the fairgrounds, DeFord stayed close by Watson.

Like most Blacks of that day, he sometimes had to put up with verbal abuse, much of it petty. On his return home from the recording session in New York, he changed trains in Saltville, Virginia. When he gave the train attendant in Saltville a dollar bill that was slightly torn, she refused to take it. "Give me a good dollar, nigger!" she exclaimed. "I didn't say a word; I just gave her a new one," he remembered.

It would be wrong to assume such incidents were ever commonplace for him. They were not. They stood out in his memory because they were actually quite rare. DeFord got along well with virtually everyone, whether white or Black. Even in the heyday of segregation, he came and went pretty much as he pleased with no problems. Personally, he rarely encountered hostility and suffered little abuse during his eighty-two years of living in the South. On the contrary, most people he met through the years were friendly and courteous to him.

DeFord knew how to relate to whites in such a manner that he would not be viewed as "pushy" or "forward." He enjoyed talking and visiting with the other Opry performers but seldom initiated these conversations: "I stayed in my place. I didn't push myself forward. If someone wanted to shake hands or talk to me, they came to me." On stage between numbers, he would merely say "thank you" to the audience and then go on to the next tune. He had a seat in one corner of the WSM studio. When he arrived every Saturday night, he went straight to his chair and sat there except to perform or go to the bathroom. (He did, by the way, use the same bathroom as the white performers.) After his part on the program was completed, "I didn't hang around. I came to perform, then I went home." His colleagues on the Opry have confirmed this. His fellow harmonica player Herman Crook noted, "DeFord never did get smart." Fiddlin' Sid Harkreader elaborated by saying, "DeFord was never out of place. You would never know he was here. He was very nice if someone talked to him. He never butted in." Kirk McGee summed it up by saying, "He would just about answer your questions."

DeFord's fellow Opry performers would have been surprised to know that, as a child, he had talked so much he was nicknamed "Talk-a-Lot" by his foster parents. His mother told him once that, since he loved to talk so much, he ought to become a lawyer. As an adult, his love of conversation was as strong as ever when he was with family or friends.

He seldom meddled in things that didn't concern him. "Let every tub set on its own bottom," was one of his favorite sayings. He saw many things on his travels that he never mentioned to anyone. Other performers could drink, carry on, or carouse, but he wouldn't say anything to them or the Opry management unless he was directly affected himself. "See and don't see, hear and don't hear," was another way he described his attitude during those times. Even when something came up that affected him, he was very circumspect about how he raised the issue. He would talk to Judge Hay about it rather than raise the issue in public. As a result of one such incident, Hay praised Bailey's example and set up regular meetings with the performers to learn of their problems. "Little DeFord ain't supposed to have an ounce of sense, but he had sense enough to come to the office when he had a problem with the show," Judge Hay told the other performers. "Let's all take after DeFord. Don't show off out in the field. If something goes wrong, come to the office."

DeFord's reticence was clearly self-imposed. In groups of white persons, he assumed a background role that Blacks in that day were expected to assume. He would sit in the corner saying little, but he wasn't deaf or dumb. "I would just play dumb like I didn't know anything, but I was soaking it in like the rain," he remembered. At times he walked a thin line. It was a necessity for him, but it limited him as a performer. As he explained it, he was "handicapped":

I could have been a better musician, but I was handicapped and I was afraid I'd do something wrong. See, white people could do wrong, they'd just do wrong. They can't do nothing with one another. . . . I knowed in my time . . . it don't work like that [for a Black man]. I held down a lot of things I could do playing on a harp, which would go over big today if I was a young man and had a place to do it. . . . I could do things, me walking, laying on the floor, turning over, turning somersaults, and still blowing the train. . . . Well, back in that time [they would have said], "Well, he's too smart. . . . . He does too much. . . ." Just like if I'd went to Detroit for that contest with that harp. They was giving away a Ford and a Lincoln. Well, I'd have got the Lincoln with just no trouble. . . . Mr. Hay said, "Don't go." Well, I thought I wouldn't have had no success [here]. I would have got the Lincoln, and come back down here and I probably wouldn't have made it with the public like I made it without that thing. . . . See what

I'm talking about? That's too much for a Black man, . . . taking a 25 cent harp to win a Lincoln. Gasoline was selling for a dime or 15 cents a gallon at that time. I was working at a tire place. . . . I could have kept my car up. . . . . I'd have had it slicked up and shined and I'd have built me a garage where I lived out of nothing and kept it in there. See, that would've been too much for a Black man at that time. I'd have ruined myself. . . .

You all ain't seen nothing. . . . It's a pity I was held down like that. I couldn't git loose. . . . I couldn't show my act. . . . I was real funny. I used to could set down on the floor with my legs straight out, . . . but I couldn't do that up there. I tell you what I knowed was slick just like me playing a harp. Well, back in them times, that was too slick for a Black man. Too smooth, they'd say. . . . I could do some terrible tricks, laying down and turning over and twisting my arms around in different shapes. I was limber and everything. . . . I'd have just been covered up with money, if people could have got to me like that and if I'd had my rights like the white people did back in that time. Oh man, I don't know how much money I'd have had . . . . I was the wrong color to git anywhere back then, yup, the wrong color.

DeFord's place among the virtually all-white country music field and Opry cast has been described in various ways. One Opry promotion flyer of the 1940s described him as "the Opry's mascot." This is easy to understand. Being Black, small, and handicapped contributed to a "mascot" image, but the term is quite misleading in that it implies he was not pulling his weight as a full performer. On the contrary, his skill, performance, and popularity clearly ranked him as a heavyweight among the performers. "We considered him a pretty strong act," Kirk McGee confirmed years later. A record album issued in the early 1970s described him as "the Opry's house nigger," a term referring to slavery days' distinction between house and field servants. "House slaves" or "house niggers" were those well-dressed, well-mannered Blacks who held the more desirable plantation positions "in the big house." Such servants were in close contact with the white family members, and close personal relationships often developed between them. There is some accuracy in this description of DeFord. Compared to many Blacks of that day, he was unusually well-dressed and well-mannered. He had a close relationship with several of the white Opry staff, including George Hay, Uncle Dave, the Delmores, and the McGees. He even worked "on the side" for Hay. But he wasn't on the Opry as a token or a symbol. He was there for the same reason they were—to produce a product much in demand by the WSM listening audience.

For some time after DeFord appeared on the Opry, there was no mention "on the air" that he was "a colored man." Many people listening to him on the radio never knew this. Often, they would learn of his race only if they saw him perform on tours or saw him on the Opry itself. This was not accidental. Judge Hay told DeFord he was afraid "they'd blow us out" if his race were publicized. As time went on, the concern proved to be groundless. Bailey's race made little difference to the listening public. He never met with any hostility or difficulties from his audiences, wherever he went. But traveling with white performers in the 1920s and 1930s did present problems for DeFord. Segregation was the custom everywhere, and in most states where DeFord traveled it was supported by law. In places it was illegal for him to stay in a hotel or eat in a restaurant that served his white colleagues. "It was rough for him in those days," Roy Acuff remembered.

To make things worse, DeFord toured many places where he felt particularly conspicuous: "I been some places with the Grand Ole Opry show where I was the first Black man that had been there since the Civil War. Some of the white children had never seen a Black man." DeFord was never hurt or molested in any physical way. "Nobody ever hurt me . . . but they'd look at me hard sometimes." He believed that he avoided many problems because of his appearance and the way he acted: "My character and looks kept me going. You know the way I carried myself. Just like a fine German Shepherd with a collar. You know somebody's behind it. They knew if something happened to me, somebody would be checking on me."

This "somebody" was obviously WSM or the National Life & Accident Insurance Company. When traveling, DeFord always made clear his association with them, since National Life, WSM, and the Grand Ole Opry were well-known almost everywhere he went. The National Life symbol—a shield—was familiar in most communities, and there were National Life agents in many of those towns. By identifying himself with the company, DeFord immediately eliminated many problems he might have encountered otherwise. One way he did this was by wearing a silver pin with the letters WSM on it. Soon after he started traveling, he had the pin made by a silversmith in downtown Nashville. He usually wore it on his lapel. It was in the shape of a shield representing the message of the station's call letters, WSM: "We Shield Millions." Its raised black letters on the silver were easily recognizable. "It spoke for me, letting people know who I was," he said. "I wore that pin for years and years."

"Cousin Wilbur" Bill Wesbrooks with Bailey wearing WSM cap.
Photograph given to Morton by Bailey for use in biography.

Still, it was tough for DeFord. It was always a problem for him to find a place to eat wherever he was, north or south. He usually had to eat in the car or at the back door of the restaurant. In a few cases, he was able to find a Black restaurant or eat in the kitchen of a white one. On several occasions, cafe owners and employees went out of their way to help him while not upsetting tradition or violating the law. He recalled a trip to Cincinnati, where he "looked for a Black restaurant and couldn't find one. I finally went in a white one and went straight to the kitchen. I told them I was hungry and couldn't find a place to eat. They fixed me up a great meal and wouldn't charge me a thing." All of his fellow performers would make certain that he got something to eat and drink, but some went beyond that. The Delmore Brothers, Alton and Rabon, were especially sensitive to his well-being:

> I enjoyed going with them, because they'd stick by me through thick and thin. They was 100 percent. They watched out for me. "If you can't feed little DeFord, we can't eat here either," I remember them saying a many a time. I usually had to eat in the kitchen, but at least they saw to it that I got to come inside to eat, and not have to set out in the car. If the place wouldn't let me come in at all, then they'd drive on down the road fifty miles or more to find another place that would. Most of the other performers would get me a sandwich and bring it to me to eat in the car, but not them boys.

Finding a place for DeFord to sleep was an even more serious problem. "That was like trying to walk without no feet," he said. Judge Hay referred to this problem in his 1949 unpublished manuscript, "The Grand Ole Opry Hits the Road": "DeFord played on the road with various acts. He is a very quiet man who gave the boys no trouble, except that it was sometimes difficult to find a place for him to stay, but that was not his fault." Only a few hotels would knowingly allow him to stay with the white performers. Often he simply went in with the group and no questions were asked. On some occasions, he was "smuggled" into the hotel room by posing as a baggage boy. Some proprietors merely looked the other way, perhaps glad to have an alibi. Uncle Dave Macon would insist that DeFord was his valet and was often able to get him in that way. Most of the cars had a seat that was removable, and Uncle Dave would have it brought into the hotel room for DeFord to use as a mattress on the floor.

If a bed or mattress was not available for him, some of the performers shared their beds with him. Bert Hutcherson remembered when he, Paul Warmack, the

Delmore Brothers, and DeFord went on a tour together, DeFord slept between the two Delmore Brothers in the same bed. Although Hutcherson was rather surprised, this was actually a common practice when DeFord traveled with the Delmore Brothers, the Vagabonds, and occasionally with Roy Acuff & the Smoky Mountain Boys. With the Vagabonds, sometimes he would sleep crossways at the foot of the bed. When hotels refused to admit him, his fellow performers would try to find him other accommodations. It was not uncommon for one or more of them to be walking down dark streets in a strange town with him, at two or three o'clock in the morning, looking for a place for him to stay. If a place looked too rough, he wouldn't stay there. "I seen some terrible places," he said. Highly conscious of his small size, he knew he would be an easy target for muggers and thieves.

He was in Virginia one night "in the dead of winter" with Honey Wilds when they couldn't find him a place to stay. The only remaining place Wilds could think of was the local jail, but DeFord adamantly refused. "I'd have been safe there, but I didn't like the sound of it, 'being in jail.' I was ready to quit. I hadn't never stayed in no jail, and I wasn't going to start then." Reluctantly, they kept looking and finally found him another place to sleep—in the lobby of the local funeral home. Kirk McGee said he could always find a Black family to take in DeFord. Other performers were not always so successful, though, and DeFord often ended up sleeping in the car. When he did this, he would "crack all the windows an inch or two and cover up with a blanket." In such circumstances, he never could sleep very well "because of dogs and wild animals" he would hear throughout the night. In cold weather, he had the added problem of trying to keep warm. He kept the heavy army blanket that he bought when he was in Wheeling, West Virginia, one cold winter in the early 1930s. He carried it with him on scores of subsequent trips.

However difficult things were for him, he almost never complained. He realized that he was fortunate to be on the Opry cast and to be traveling around the country with a group of white performers. In fact, he often joked about his uniqueness as the only "colored" or Black person on the Opry cast: "One Saturday night me and Mr. Roy Acuff was up at WSM. We lay up there in the window. Some ladies, two or three of them, asked, 'Which one are you?' Mr. Roy said, 'I'm one of them.' When he said that, I said, 'And I'm the blackest one of them.' They laughed. I've been a mess. I'm telling you the truth."

In the early 1930s, in an attempt to add color to the visual side of the show, Judge Hay asked the musicians to dress up in hayseed style, with overalls. DeFord's reaction was, "I told them I didn't need no costume. I was a costume just like I was." DeFord usually found some humor in even the most awkward situations:

One time I was in Myrtle Beach, playing with Roy Acuff and his band. They all was out there in the ocean swimming. That was the first time I'd saw the Atlantic Ocean. Just to say I've been in it, I rolled my britches legs up and walked out in it. When I walked out, a policeman came up to me. He said, "John Henry, colored folks go swimming about eighteen miles up." I said, "Anybody fool enough to go in that ocean, you ought to let them go in any place they want." Everybody laughed.

It was fortunate that DeFord could laugh about such situations. Otherwise, it would have been even more difficult for him to deal with them. On the one hand, he was lauded and cheered by white audiences and eagerly sought out by promoters and performers; on the other hand, he had to endure all sorts of things merely because of his color. On stage he was an equal to the other performers, but off stage he couldn't go with them into a restaurant or a hotel lobby no matter how well he was dressed, how clean he was, or how much money he had. A white man could go in such places no matter how untalented, dirty, or poorly dressed he was. While he said nothing about these things to anyone, they left their mark on the sensitive DeFord. He had no choice but to go along with the system, but he knew it wasn't right:

This is a great big world, but, you know, I ain't never been free. Even now, I can't go in restaurant without worrying about whether I should go in or not. I been to places with Honey Wilds where they would not sell him a sandwich for me. I didn't suffer, but I was handicapped. I been penned up all my life. You got to know how to take it and go on.

That's gone now, but I still can't feel welcome in restaurants, if I don't see no Black folks in there. I'm not against white folks. It's just the way I had to live for so long.

Though he couldn't forget it, he didn't think it was helpful to dwell on the injustices or problems of the past. He questioned the wisdom of showing programs on television like *Roots*, because they might make young Blacks today "try to get even" for injustices of the past. "Them days is gone," he said. "We need to look at the future, not the past." Moreover, he thought it was wrong to hold one person responsible for what another person did years ago. "You can't blame somebody now for what their grandpa did," he philosophized.

"We all need to work together, not against each other," he said. "We need each other." As he explained to me in 1980 during the Iranian hostage crisis:

> Now the Black is got to fight for the white and the white got to fight for the Black. They got to learn to understand that. You and me might be dead and gone, but we Black people got to fight for your son someday, if he lives long enough. He may have a family and all that. We may have to fight for him someday. We got to learn to stick to each other. So this other way we been living is wrong. . . .
>
> By we [Blacks] not having nothing, we just like your little son, he can't do nothing for himself. We're in the same shape and we're grown. We have no money, no power, no machines, no guns or no nothing. We have to do what the man says do. See what I'm talking about. This has got to be our home. We're here, we can't get away. We can't walk out.
>
> They're mad at the white man. They want everything to be equal. Well, that equal's all right, but they're bringing it down in the wrong attitude. You got to understand that equal business. You see, equal rights mean more than it sounds like. Equal rights is a whole lot. It's a big word like I tell you. It takes a sensible man to have equal rights and use equal rights in this case and break it down right. And then the world will be better.

"We all need to have the right kind of values in our heart," he said. "Keep a clean heart for yourself and when you got a clean heart for yourself, you got a clean heart for everybody else."

Where DeFord could control things, he was ahead of his time. When he was renting rooms in his home on Lafayette Street, he rented to whoever wanted to stay with him, white or Black. He had numerous white people who stayed overnight in one of his rooms, and often he had whites in one room and Blacks in another at the same time. Though DeFord was never officially licensed as a motel operator, for several years he operated what was in effect Nashville's first integrated motel.

There was a single, rather frightening occurrence one night in 1937 or 1938, apparently in response to his renting of rooms to both Blacks and whites. DeFord never spoke of this, but DeFord Jr. remembers it vividly. His father was out of town on a tour. He and his mother awakened to find a burning cross in their front yard. For the next few nights they had male relatives from both sides of the family stay with them, but nothing else occurred, and DeFord continued to rent to all comers.

His shoeshine shop was always open to both Blacks and whites: "White people would stop and say, 'DeFord, can we get shined in your shop?' I'd say 'Yeah, anywhere I got something to sell, I'm selling to everybody. If I can't sell to you, I don't want to be here.' And they'd laugh."

Largely because of his radio fame, whites came in large numbers to seek him out wherever his shop was located. He welcomed them on an equal basis with his Black customers, all sitting side by side and waiting their turns: "I didn't have you sit here and I sit here. . . . Back in '33, I had them together. . . . White man walk in, seat; another walk in, seat; Black man walk in, seat; and went on. Come in and come on back. . . . We'd knock them on out and that's it. I don't care who you was. . . . I just shined shoes and didn't make me no difference. Everybody went."

How was he able to accomplish this? He thought that his music was the key:

A white barber asked me one time how I could mix them up in my shoe-shine shop and using the same seat. He said they'd run him out of town if he did that. Well I said, "They all know me and all want to hear the same tune."

His musical skills and fame clearly set DeFord apart in the eyes of many white southerners. Whites who wouldn't think of going into other Black establishments would come to his shoeshine shop. Some would even stay overnight in his home just to get a chance to hear him play his harmonica. In the process, they would use the same facilities that were used by Blacks without objection. They, along with DeFord's Black customers, "all wanted to hear the same tune."

11

"They Turned Me Loose to Root Hog or Die"

In the spring of 1941, DeFord was beginning his sixteenth season with the Opry. He was still appearing on the program as much as or more than any other regular performer—thirty weeks in 1939—but, like all the others by now, he had been cut back to one set per show. He had settled into a regular fifteen-minute slot at 9:15 P.M., just after the Fruit Jar Drinkers and just before the pop-oriented fare of Ford Rush and the blackface team of Jamup & Honey. By now the Opry had been on the NBC network for eighteen months, in carefully scripted thirty-minute segments sponsored by products like Prince Albert Smoking Tobacco. DeFord appeared on a few of these, about the only time he had a nationwide network venue, but most of the network air time went to new Opry stars like Roy Acuff and Minnie Pearl. The balance of the typical Opry show—the non-network portion—still included many of the old-time acts that had been on the show from its start: the Crook Brothers, Uncle Dave Macon, the McGee Brothers, the Fruit Jar Drinkers, the Gully Jumpers, and Robert Lunn. The slick "uptown" acts that had arrived in the mid-1930s—such as Clayton McMichen's Georgia Wildcats, Curly Fox & Texas Ruby, and Pee Wee King's Golden West Cowboys—had moved on, and for a time the show had retrenched, going back to its tried-and-true grassroots appeal. Yet to come were the new revolutionary sounds of people like Ernest Tubb, Eddy Arnold, and Red Foley. The show had an old-time ambiance that, in the spring of 1941, seemed ideally suited to DeFord's music.

Nor had DeFord lost any of his appeal, or his ability to draw crowds. When Acuff joined the show in 1938, he often worked with Bailey to take advantage of the harmonica player's popularity. He recalls: "When I came to WSM in 1938,

Cast of the WSM Grand Ole Opry, with Bailey on left behind WSM Grand Ole Opry sign. Photograph given to Morton by Bailey for use in biography.

I was an unknown person. At that time, DeFord was a very popular entertainer. There was quite a demand to see him. I carried him with me because they wanted to see him. They didn't know me. We always had very nice crowds." "DeFord was pretty hot when we came down here," adds Beecher Kirby, known as "Bashful Brother Oswald" in Acuff's band. "The audiences loved him." Bill Monroe, who joined the show in October 1939 as the newest kid on the block, also took DeFord with him to help draw crowds. Far from being a token or "mascot," DeFord in 1941 was still a powerful attraction for Opry road shows, as well as being a full-fledged member of the radio cast, with his own fifteen-minute spot still very much intact. It was all the more puzzling, then, when DeFord was suddenly fired by the Opry in late May 1941.

Just why DeFord was fired from the show has for years remained somewhat of a mystery, and one of the most controversial aspects of Opry history. The modern Opry souvenir history and picture books simply avoid any mention of the incident, as do "authorized" histories such as Jack Hurst's *Grand Old Opry* (1975). Others writing about Nashville and the Opry have been less circumspect in attempting to get to the bottom of the firing. Frye Gaillard, in his book *Race, Rock, and Religion* (1982), asserts that DeFord was "dropped from the cast under cloudy circumstances" and refers to the Nashville music industry that "shafted him." Paul Hemphill, whose *The Nashville Sound* (1970) was one of the first serious portraits of modern Nashville, quotes DeFord as saying he "left" the Opry because "I wasn't getting but $4 or $5 a night, and they kept me standing in the back." Peter Guralnick, in his *Lost Highway* (1979), argues that DeFord's leaving came about because, "as the Opry became more and more the province of professional entertainers," the "anomaly of DeFord's position became increasingly evident." He also felt DeFord was getting less and less playing time, but that, in sum, to DeFord "the debacle remains a bitter puzzle to this day." Then there is the famous explanation offered by Judge Hay himself, in his book *A Story of the Grand Ole Opry* (1945):

> That brings us to DeFord Bailey, a little crippled colored boy who was a bright feature of our show for about fifteen years. Like some members of his race and other races, DeFord was lazy. He knew about a dozen numbers, which he put on the air and recorded for a major company, but he refused to learn any more, even though his reward was great. He was our mascot and is still loved by the entire company. We gave him a whole

year's notice to learn some more tunes, but he would not. When we were forced to give him his final notice, DeFord said, without malice: "I knowed it wuz comin', Judge, I knowed it wuz comin'.'"

DeFord comes to the show now and then to visit us. We are always glad to see him—a great artist.

Needless to say, DeFord didn't remember it quite this way. While he strongly rejected Hay's explanation, he didn't especially blame Hay for saying it:

He had a boss, too. It was the company. It's terrible for a company to say things like that about me. That I didn't know no songs. I reads between the lines. They seen the day was coming when they'd have to pay me right . . . and they used the excuse about me playing the same old tunes.

The charge that DeFord refused to learn any new songs is curious and complex, and deserves closer examination. DeFord admitted readily that he tended to play a certain body of tunes over and over on the Opry: "It Ain't Gonna Rain No Mo'," "Shoe Shine Boy Blues," "Lost John," "John Henry," "Ice Water Blues," "Old Hen Cackle," "Hesitation Mama," "Alcoholic Blues," "Casey Jones," "Muscle Shoals Blues," "Fox Chase," "Evening Prayer Blues," and his train pieces. And it was true that many of these had been learned in his youth, remaining in his repertoire for years. But this was due, in part, to insistence by the Opry management that he play only certain types of tunes on the show. As DeFord remembers:

I told 'em years ago I got tired of the same thing, of blowing that same thing, but I had to go along with 'em, you know. Gene Austin [the well-known pop crooner of the 1920s] played one Saturday night when I was there. Played "Blue Heaven" on his guitar. Well, I came back next week and had that down on my harp. They said, "No. Naw, don't play that. That's their song. You play blues like you've been playing."

I couldn't grow. They'd play my songs, if they wanted. That was all right If they had let me play like I wanted, I could have stole the show. If I had been a white man, I could have done it. They held me down. . . . I wasn't free.

In view of all this, DeFord could not understand why, in the 1940–41 season, "all of a sudden" the Opry management reversed this policy 180 degrees and began talking about him coming up with "brand new" tunes—not new versions of old tunes but entirely new compositions. For years this puzzled fans and historians as well. Hay implies that the demand simply reflected the "modernization" of the show, but, as we have seen, the 1941 schedule was still full of very traditional acts. Hay was vague about the real reason, which was much more ugly and controversial; it was only years later, when Opry star Kirk McGee pointed it out, that researchers were led to it: the BMI-ASCAP copyright war that broke out in 1940 and led to a boycott by radio stations of some of the country's most familiar songs.

ASCAP (the American Society of Composers, Authors, and Publishers) had been formed in 1914 as an organization devoted to making theaters, dance halls, and restaurants pay fees for the live performance of copyrighted music. After a series of favorable court decisions, and after the organization had grown to include most of the major music publishers and composers, it extended its purview to radio. In 1932, it demanded that radio pay fees geared not to its use of specific music, but to a percentage of its total income. Their reasoning was that music was by then taking up some 65 percent or more of the air time, that broadcasters were spending only 3.4 percent of their income on it, and that they were making a killing by charging sponsors high rates for commercials. Furthermore, it was argued, radio had seriously affected sales of sheet music, phonograph records, and even pianos. A contract for a flat fee of $4.5 million a year had been negotiated with the major radio networks in 1932, and in 1940 that contract was coming up for renewal. ASCAP was asking for exactly double the amount for the new contract, and the radio networks refused. The deadline for the new contract was January 1, 1941, and in the fall of 1940, with the deadline approaching, the tension was rising. Newspapers were full of stories about the networks' plans to boycott ASCAP songs and about what impact the restrictions would have on the music of the day. Radio singers and band leaders were especially concerned; Bing Crosby, quoted in *Metronome* magazine in October 1940, said that he would simply quit radio after December 31 if "denied free choice in picking material." Many big band leaders felt the same way.

To counter the loss of ASCAP material, the radio broadcasters organized a rival organization, Broadcast Music Incorporated (BMI). BMI invited songwriters who had not been allowed to join ASCAP, either because they were too young or because they specialized in country music (i.e., wrote and performed by ear), to join with them and provide a new catalog of music designed primarily for radio work. By the end of 1940, BMI claimed to have 140,000 numbers in its catalog, though only a few were actually hits. (Later, country songs like "You Are My Sunshine" and "Pistol Packin' Mama" would become some of the new organization's biggest hits.) BMI had signed contracts with over 400 radio stations, including the three main Nashville stations, WLAC, WSIX, and WSM. One of the 600 original stockholders in BMI was WSM's Edwin Craig, who was especially keen to see the new organization succeed. He made it clear that performers on his station were expected to do their part by creating new songs that could be copyrighted and licensed through BMI. As the January 1, 1941, deadline approached, the pressure become more intense. On September 21, 1940, NBC (of which WSM was an affiliate) ruled that "orchestras broadcasting on NBC sustaining shows must schedule and play at least three compositions not controlled by ASCAP during each broadcast period after October 1." The idea was to start easing the artist into using BMI material, thereby showing ASCAP that the networks and stations were serious about the boycott.

The ASCAP catalog did not just extend to current Broadway show tunes, movie hits, or big band favorites; it went far back into the fabric of American pop music. It included such basic songs as "Happy Birthday to You," "Rock-a-Bye-Baby," "Take Me Out to the Ball Game," "My Wild Irish Rose," "St. Louis Blues" (and most of W. C. Handy's other blues), "Sweet Adeline," and gospel favorites like "The Old Rugged Cross," "Go Down, Moses," "In the Garden," and "Swing Low, Sweet Chariot." Though some of these, and many others in the ASCAP catalog, were in fact traditional folk songs, over the years they had been dutifully copyrighted by various composers who had done arrangements of them. In the 1920s and 1930s, for instance, Ralph Peer, the Victor talent scout and A&R man who had recorded DeFord in Nashville back in 1928, routinely filed copyrights on just about any song he recorded for Victor and "published" it with his Southern Music—an ASCAP affiliate. DeFord's music, therefore, was bound to be affected by the ASCAP ban.

The threats became reality on January 1, 1941, when the boycott went into effect. Across the country, radio fans and critics alike began complaining about the sudden influx of odd, unfamiliar tunes, and the hastily contrived dance-band arrangements of classical pieces like Glenn Miller's "Song of the Volga Boatmen" or "Anvil Chorus." Jazz musicians were forbidden to take solos, and improvising of any sort was forbidden; the feeling was that a soloist might unconsciously "quote" from a copyrighted ASCAP song. (This, as we will see, was especially applicable to DeFord, who often improvised in his solos.) In Nashville, men like Opry music librarian Vito Pellettieri had begun to check out songs Opry personnel wanted to play and began finding out that many old favorites had ASCAP copyrights. This included many of the blues pieces that DeFord played, as well as his famous "Fox Chase," which had been copyrighted by Henry Whitter and Southern Music back in the 1920s. DeFord remembered: "You know the tune 'Casey Jones'? I had played it for years. Other people had, too. One night somebody called in and said that song was restricted and nobody could play it on the Opry no more."

This, then, was the explanation for Hay's curious comment about the Opry giving DeFord "a whole year's notice" to "learn some more tunes." He was especially hard hit by the ASCAP ban; many of his best songs were unusable on the air. It did not matter that many of the tunes were old traditional ones that DeFord had known since childhood; some kind of copyright did exist on them, and with WSM just beginning to make inroads with getting the Opry on the network, nobody wanted to alienate NBC.

DeFord felt caught between a rock and a hard place. For years he had been "restricted" to a rather small repertoire of tunes on the show, and now suddenly he was being asked to come up with new ones. To further complicate matters, his very notion of what it took to make a good tune was different from that of most other Opry musicians, or many of the dance-band musicians on the networks. His approach was not to learn a tune and then repeatedly play it in a fixed form. His approach was to improve or perfect a tune he liked, playing it in countless ways, trying notes and tones one way, then another. "It takes years to make a good tune," he said. This is something "Black people know" but "most white people don't."

White people think Black people are the best musicians in the world. That's 'cause they make us play. They feel like they can't. They could if they would, but they want to get through it too quick. It takes years of your life on one song.

See, they'll write a hundred songs. There won't be enough words out of all of 'em to make one perfect, good, nice song. . . . They're in a hurry. They'll pick on one thing, one key note, and that's it. They'll go over the top. They'll say, "Well, I made $5,000 tonight. What's the need to worry any more about that one?" They'll write some more. They're gone on then, and they ain't played n'er song. They just got a whole lot of songs out there. You get that melody out of there, them off-notes like I know how to place them, you have nothing. You won't make n'er whole song. I play a song over and over and over.

By me playing the harp, I had such a good sound. . . . I could change a sound so, I could come up with fine notes. Folks would say, "I'd rather hear him play that." . . . Just like being a good dancer: Black or white, everybody would say, "Let him dance." You could not be a good dancer, but be such a good comedian or funny, you'd go over better than the one that danced.

See, you have a pull one way or the other. I had a pull one way, and changed my notes. Whatever I played, it had such a mellow and peculiar sound. Like a man preaching.

In short, DeFord was very much aware that he was a stylist rather than a creator of new songs. This is one of the reasons he wasn't too upset when other Opry performers occasionally performed one of "his" songs; the performance would be so different stylistically that it might as well be another tune. Unfortunately, the ASCAP-BMI rules made little provision for stylistics; indeed, by banning any musical improvisation from the air, the radio networks struck another blow against DeFord's music since much of what was uniquely "his" about a tune was improvised. He was thus being challenged on two levels, in a complex situation over which he had no control and which he didn't fully understand. In fact, DeFord went so far as to associate "new songs" with "new style." He explained, "It's like working on cars. I worked on one style for sixteen years. Then they tried to get me to play another one. I was sixteen years behind." Hurt, puzzled, offended, he responded by continuing to perform just as he always had, bearing it all in dignified silence. "I've been through rough times, but I kept my head out of water and kept paddling. I don't let nothing get me down."

The weekly radio listings in the Nashville newspapers show that the end finally came in late May 1941. After May 24, DeFord's name no longer appeared in the listings. Not coincidentally, his departure came at the height of the ASCAP boycott, five months into the total ban of all ASCAP songs. By the end of July, NBC, WSM's network, would sign an agreement with ASCAP, and things would be pretty much returned to normal—for everyone, that is, except DeFord Bailey. Alcyone Bate Beasley, the daughter of DeFord's old friend and mentor, Dr. Humphrey Bate, noted the irony of the situation. On today's Opry, and on the Opry for generations, most performers do "exactly what DeFord was let go for. They play the tunes they are best known for. Who can imagine Roy Acuff on the Opry not playing either 'Wabash Cannonball' or 'Great Speckled Bird'?"

Bailey in the 1930s. Photograph given to Morton by Bailey for use in biography.

DeFord did not remember the exact date of his last Opry show in 1941. He did remember, though, that the management was so sensitive to his firing that, for several weeks after he left the show, they continued to pay him to come on down to the broadcast just to "be around and let people see me." He thought this was an effort to quiet public criticism over his firing: "The people talked about it a whole lot, about not treating me right. They called me back up there to be around and let people see me. They'd give me $3 a night. I went about three times. Finally, I decided to quit. I didn't want no more of that."

In addition to the insult to his music and his professionalism, the firing was a serious blow to DeFord in practical terms. He was forty-two years old, a little late in life to be starting a new career; and he had a wife and three young children aged nine, seven, and five: "They turned me loose with a wife and kids to root hog or die. They didn't give a hoot which way I went. They got the good out of me and turned me loose." Some forty years after the incident, DeFord still resented how the station had treated him. "Sometimes I wish I'd never heard of WSM," he said. "They made me have some bad thoughts, and I don't like that." For years he said he did not have one thing in his house he could "thank WSM for."

He did not blame Judge Hay for it all; he sensed that by then Hay was losing power with the Opry management and that circumstances were beyond his control: "Judge Hay did all he could. If he'd helped me, he'd have lost his job too. At that time, a white man couldn't do too much for a Black person. If they did, they wouldn't get any help. It was nationwide. I was a Black man."

At the same time, DeFord knew of numerous employers in Nashville who took a personal interest in the welfare of their employees and provided various fringe benefits for them. DeFord once expected as much from the Opry, but after 1941 he felt that the Opry's top management had no real concern at all for him or any of the employees. A story DeFord told about the Opry's Christmas tree seemed to symbolize his continual disappointment:

They'd have a Christmas tree every Christmas Eve night. When it came on Saturday night, I'd be there. That was our work night, you know. I didn't ever get nothing off that Christmas tree. I never could figure that out. That's the only thing I never could figure out. I know if you work for the poorest sort of people, colored or white, around Christmas they're going to give you something. If you work for a man that's got a fairly good living, you can't tote all your stuff home at night. But . . . I ain't got nothing. I couldn't figure it out. The thing would be full of stuff. . . . I ain't got a nickel. There wasn't ever nothing for me. They'd have that tree every year. . . .

I asked one time why I never got a Christmas card. They told me it would cost too much.

12

"I Knowed I Could Make It on My Own"

DeFord had lived in or near the Edgehill section of Nashville ever since he came to town in 1918. At that time, the area was called "Rocktown," and like many Black neighborhoods of the day, it was "a rough place to live." Some parts were so dangerous they had become the stuff of legend. As Bailey recalled, "There was one alley, behind Thirteenth Avenue, that was called Amen Alley. If you made it through at night, you said 'Amen.' It was really rough." There were four main Black neighborhoods in Nashville in these days, and a lot of crosstown rivalry. "If somebody from north Nashville went out south, they'd run 'em back," he remembered, and youngsters had to become skilled at rock fighting. Kids even learned special techniques such as the use of "sailers," rocks thrown deliberately high in the air to divert opponents' attention from the real threat. "They'd throw sailers up high, then quickly throw a fast straight one to hit him while he was looking for the first one to come down." Black and white schools followed staggered schedules to prevent children from getting on the streets at the same time and fighting. It was a testimony to DeFord's popularity, though, that he could go into any of the sections whenever he wanted to. "I could go anywhere in town without any problems," he recalled.

This popularity and street savvy would take on a new meaning for DeFord in the summer of 1941, after he left the Opry. The experience was traumatic, but it was also a watershed in his life. He resolved that, whatever the difficulties, he would never again work for anybody else. From there on, he would make it on his own: "Mr. Hay told me I would 'starve to death in Edgehill with them niggers,' but I told him, 'I'm gonna try.' When they turned me out, I didn't have a cent, but I had sense. I knowed I could make it on my own. I walked out of WSM with a smile. I told myself, 'God gave every man five senses and I'm going to use them. I ain't gonna work for another man as long as I live.' I'd work for myself."

Never one to reject menial work, he immediately turned his attention to alternative ways of making a decent living for himself and his young family:

I made the back room of my house on Thirteenth Avenue South into a shoeshine parlor and shined shoes for a dime. Later on, when I lived on Grand Avenue, I had the shop in the front room.

While living on Thirteenth Avenue, I [also] cooked dinners and sold 'em to workmen at R. H. Lee's coal yard at Eleventh and Twelfth avenues near Union Station. I got me a wagon, heated bricks and put 'em in the bottom. Put asbestos coating on 'em. Then put food on top of the bricks and covered it all up. I'd sell the food hot to the workmen at twelve noon. Mr. Lee himself bought from me.

I also got to buying some coal from them that I'd sell and carry to other people. When they had that real cold winter back in 1951, most people couldn't get coal. I could have charged a lot for what I had then, but I still sold it cheap. I couldn't take advantage of people like that. I had a ton of coal in my shop. I even slept there at night some of the time so I could sell it to people whenever they needed it.

For a time, things were tough. "I had a hard time," he admitted, "but I didn't let it bluff me." He managed to take care of his family throughout it all. "The welfare people came out wanting to help me. I told them no. I wanted to take care of myself. They talked with me for a long time. Told me to call 'em if I ever needed to. I never did."

While running his shoeshine shop, DeFord sold various things to eat there: popcorn, soft drinks, candy, ice cream, even fruit. He had a "fancy $1,800 popcorn machine" that he had bought second-hand from a local insurance salesman for about a hundred dollars. In good weather, he set it just outside the front door to the shop and had his shoeshine boys tend to it. "People would buy popcorn," he nodded. "Nickel and dime, quarter, you'd be surprised how that will add up."

But his main concern in the years following 1941 was clearly the shoeshine business itself. Many Blacks of DeFord's reputation would have looked on such a business as representing one of the more repugnant Black stereotypes, but not DeFord. He needed to keep busy and had no qualms about the kind of work he did. He first started shining shoes when he was still on the Opry in the 1930s and making a fairly good income from music. Often, though, he found himself with time on his hands during the weekdays. "They asked me, 'Why do you want to shine shoes?' I told 'em I didn't want to be standing on a corner or on somebody's porch."

He had shined his first pair of shoes when he was a boy on the farm and had nothing for polish except chimney soot. He learned how to "spit shine" working on his own shoes, and he was able to use this skill when he was a houseboy working on West End Avenue or in the various mansions of Nashville. By then he was learning how to shine with the best available waxes and polishes. He had set up his first shoeshine business in 1933 in a barbershop operated by one of his uncles, George Reedy. Possibly because of his Opry fame, he was not required to have a city license for this shop. For years he kept a letter from an official in the City License Department, one R. B. Jackson, dated September 22, 1933, testifying that he didn't "need a city license to shine shoes in a Barber Shop and Parlor."

After he left the Opry, he went into the shoeshining business full time. He soon found that he didn't have to advertise; many of his customers already knew how skilled he was at this. "My hand moves like a machine when I'm working on shoes," he explained, and he delighted in creating a high-quality gloss on his shoes. One of his regular customers was a doctor who told him that he handled a shoe like a doctor handled a patient. Soon he had more business that he could handle by himself, and before long he had two or three others working with him. For many years, when he was located on Twelfth Avenue South, he had an elaborate setup with nine chairs and as many personnel, in addition to a spray machine.

The only sign he had outside the shop was one showing the price of a shoeshine, but his customers were always able to find him. "I run a shop all them years and I never put my name on the window. Folks would look for me. I'd move and they'd find me. I just put the price of a shine up, and sometimes I didn't even put that up." He did have two signs that were invariably posted on the inside of the shop wherever he had moved to. One was a poem:

STOP HERE,
GET YOUR SHOES SHINED QUICK,
BOSTON SLICK,
DUST WON'T STICK,
STOP HERE.
GET YOURS SHINED QUICK.
YOU'RE NEXT.

Bailey with a sign placed in his shoeshine shop. Photograph by Archie E. Allen.

The other was an admonition:

NO LOAFING OR STRONG BEVERAGES ALLOWED.

Because of his location in Edgehill, he had more Black customers than white ones. There were, though, a large number of whites who regularly came to him, even if they had to go miles out of their way.

I had white people come from Lebanon, Clarksville, Franklin, Columbia, and everywhere to shine their shoes.

I shined all kind of shoes. I shined shoes that cost $175: shoes, boots, $175 handmade. I shined all grades of shoe, and them $175 boots I have laid down on. I shined some so good that people [would] give me $5 and say keep the change. Oh, I can lay down on a pair of shoes.

I shined 'em and dyed 'em. People would buy a brand new pair of shoes and come in wanting me to dye them another color. I was that good. I could make 'em wine, beige, bone. I had a spraying machine and everything. I could dye a pair of shoes before they could go to town and back. I'd have 'em waiting for 'em.

DeFord outside his shoeshine shop. Photograph given to Morton by Bailey for use in biography.

Some people would even mail shoes to him to shine, and others would bring in their shoes before they went on vacation. "I had some bring 'em from Detroit and New York here sometimes on their vacation and bring three or four dozen. . . . Why, I've had as high as thirty-five, forty, and fifty pairs of shoes sitting around shined, ready to go. That's right. I shined as high as $50 and $75 worth of shoes a day, a many a time."

With money, DeFord displayed the same caution in his shoeshine shop that he had shown in traveling around the country with Opry tour groups. Worried about being robbed, he was careful "not to show no money; if someone handed him a large bill that required change, he would always have someone take it to a nearby store to get change. "I could have $20 worth of change in my pocket, but I'd always send the runner for change; I didn't ever give no change myself." Then, of course, he still had "Old Bessie," his pistol, which Roy Acuff called his "artillery," as a form of insurance; his employees and many of his customers knew he carried it, and this may have been one reason why he never had to use it.

He soon became a father figure to some of the boys in his tough neighborhood. He did not like for them to carry guns themselves because many didn't know how to handle them, and they were generally "hot-headed." He pointed out, "If they're nervous, they'll do things they shouldn't."

Bailey's shoes and the metal megaphone he had made for touring with other Opry performers. Photograph by David Morton.

When youngsters came into his shop with guns they wanted to sell, he would buy them just to get the weapons out of circulation. He never parted with guns he thus acquired, and years later he told me, "I bet I could shoot 400, 500 times with what I got here." His advice to other boys who were "fooling around" with guns was to take them home or get rid of them. Years later, some of these men, then grown, came to DeFord to tell him how much they appreciated his taking an interest in them; they said he treated them like a real father would. DeFord remembered: "Those boys treated me like a preacher. They wouldn't fight in front of me. I could handle 'em even though they were twice as big as me. Anybody hear me talk would think I was a preacher."

Unlike some performers who left the Opry and easily made the transition to other radio or touring work, DeFord never really tried seriously to maintain his musical career. His public appearances did not completely end, but they fell off dramatically; he continued to play his harmonica for family, friends, and customers, but tours and shows became fewer and fewer. For a time, he continued to do an occasional tour with people like Bill Monroe, but an incident that happened during the war made him even more suspicious of WSM and the Opry.

DeFord was invited to be in a film that was being made to boost the morale of U.S. armed forces overseas. One of a number of such films made by various entertainment-industry figures, this one was to feature members of the Opry cast. The day for the filming was set, and DeFord returned to the old Ryman Auditorium, where the Opry had moved shortly after he left it. He spent the entire afternoon there, from one to seven o'clock, and was filmed playing several tunes. He was then filmed clowning around with some of the other musicians; at one point, he recalled, "two big guys, Flatt and Scruggs, had me hold my hands stiff and lifted me up as a joke." All in all, it was a pleasant enough experience, and to boot he got a payment of $50 for his day's work. He was happy enough with this until later on when he found that other stars on the program had been paid $1,000. Feeling that he had contributed as much to the film as anyone else, he was upset to learn that he had received only a fraction of what they had been paid. The film was in fact shown to GIs all over the world, and after the war some of his former shoeshine boys came by to report that they had seen him in the film "in China," but this was cold comfort. (Roy Acuff also remembered the filming; if any prints survive, they would provide an invaluable record not only of DeFord performing in his prime, but of the early Opry in general.) In 1967, DeFord was filmed again, performing two numbers for the black-and-white syndicated film series, *National Life's Grand Ole Opry*. His two numbers, "Fox Chase" and "Pan American Blues," were used on separate installments of the show in the fall of 1967, and one was later issued on a 1988 Grand Ole Opry videotape, *Legends of the Grand Ole Opry*. But as often as the films were run, they seemed to DeFord yet another instance of exploitation, making him even more determined not to return to WSM. If he would not be treated fairly for his efforts, he would rather not perform at all. "Just because I banged by head once don't mean I have to keep doing it," he explained.

What little performing he did do in the ten years after the war was confined to other Nashville radio or television stations. For a time in the early 1950s, he did appear regularly on a local television program sponsored by Rainbow Cleaners; in fact, he was playing for them on the day that his old touring companion, Uncle Dave Macon, died in 1952.

In 1950–51, he toured the rural schoolhouse circuit with WLAC bluegrass star Carl Tipton and Roy Acuff band member Rachel Veach. During this time, too, he was pleased to see his three children begin singing gospel music in local churches as the Bailey Trio; he occasionally performed with them. When one of his daughters, Christine, moved to Chicago to become a schoolteacher, he visited her, making his only out-of-town performances during this time. The first of these wasn't even planned; he and his daughter had gone to watch a Chicago radio show hosted by Don McNeil, the well-known *Breakfast Club*. There DeFord was recognized and was asked to play on the program the next day. He agreed, and was paid $100 for his efforts. He went over so well that later on the station asked him to come back and paid him the same fee, plus transportation and expenses to Chicago.

Through all of this, DeFord maintained the distinctive image he had cultivated from his earliest days on the Opry and in the public eye: quiet dignity, neatness, and sharp appearance. Even during the hard times that followed his leaving the Opry, he always managed to dress well in what he called "quality" clothing, which he always kept in excellent condition. When he was a child, suffering through his various health problems, he told his mother that, if he lived to be grown, he'd "dress up every day." "You'll work, then," she replied. Without hesitation, he answered, "Yes ma'am, I'll work." And he did. As a performer, he soon realized that a good appearance was important; he knew that nice, well-fitting clothes improved his stage image and made his physical deformity less obvious. Years later, veteran Opry stars who worked with DeFord were still able to remember how well he dressed. Roy Acuff's dobro player, "Oswald" Kirby, remembers that DeFord usually wore "a blue serge suit, a white shirt, and a bow tie," and that his "clothes were as clean as a dang pin." Some noted that DeFord actually dressed better than others on the show, especially during the time when there was a move afoot to have Opry stars dress up in overalls and gingham shirts. As DeFord recalled, "When I went into a hotel to work, I looked like one of the bosses."

Unlike country stars of a later age, DeFord never went in for flashy or gaudy outfits. He preferred a simple, standard style. "My hats and most of my clothes are the kind that never go out of style," he said. After he left the Opry and set up his shoeshine shop, he found he could pick up bargains in clothes from some of his young employees; they would spend nearly all their money on clothes but wear them only a few times. DeFord knew quality goods when he saw them and, when offered a chance to buy from some of his employees or customers, he looked over the goods carefully, finding that he could stretch his slender income even further by buying some of the clothes and altering them. "Since I was so little," he said, "I could always take 'em up and make 'em fit me." He had learned to sew as a child; by now he had become an accomplished tailor. In fact, he could have easily made his living as one. The most discerning eye would have had trouble distinguishing between the suits he bought "as is" and the ones he "made to fit." Clothes were simply important to him, and he felt that anyone who wished to could have good clothes: "A feller asked me how I dressed so well with as little money as I have. I said to him, 'When you go out on Saturday night for a nice time, how much do you spend?' He said, 'Ten to twenty dollars.' I said, 'That's gone when you get home, ain't it? If you spend that same money on nice clothes and shoes, you'd have some nice things to show for your money.' It's not how much money you have, but how you use it."

Over the years, DeFord amassed a huge wardrobe. At his death, he had between thirty and forty suits, about as many sports coats and slacks, twenty-five to thirty hats, and a vast quantity of gloves, vests, sweaters, belts, and other items. Many of these items were twenty to thirty years old, but they looked as good as new because of the care DeFord took with them. His hats were especially interesting, ranging from simple straw to the finest felt. He had Stetsons, Adamses, Beavers (Calgary), and Resistols (Western). One of his favorites was a brown Stetson Royal Playboy, size 6 7/8, that he bought from Joseph Frank & Son, a Nashville clothier. He compared his Resistol self-conforming Western hat with those that Hank Snow, the Canadian Opry singer, wore. He had bought his oldest hat in 1951; it was a pure white hat, "the Texan," with a small green and yellow feather in the side. He remembered paying $8.85 for it at a shop in the old Arcade in downtown Nashville. His hats ranged in colors from gray to yellow, from pink to eggshell to olive. He kept each of his twenty-five to thirty hats in plastic bags or hat boxes. If he stayed in the house long enough to pull his hat off, he did not put it down until he "had it in plastic."

By such careful ways, DeFord was able to structure a new life for himself in the 1940s and 1950s. He was able to survive an event that could have been a serious blow to his ego, to his identity, and to his self-sufficiency. In spite of his loss of any regular venue, he was still very much a public figure. He had turned his physical appearance into one of his most notable features. In later years, he observed:

It tickles me the way folks look at me when I go somewhere. They can't believe how I dress. . . . Sometimes, I put that shoe on and a suit and a hat and I walk in H. G. Hills grocery store. They just looking. Maybe somebody will say, "That's DeFord, I thought that was somebody. Look at him. Ain't he dressed?" They'll look. Sometimes I got on a cowboy hat. They shake their head and they just wonder how on earth. . . . They can't understand. Me being a Black man with that kind of stuff on. They know when they see something.

I say, "Yeah, this is me," and I done gone about my business. This shoe'll look like a mirror. . . . Good tie on. Good everything.

Don't have nothing short. The only thing I want to be short is me. Let me be short, don't let my clothes be short.

13

"We Got to Meet Jesus Someday"

Deford Bailey was a very moral and religious man. His religious faith was based on traditional Christian teachings. He made every effort to live his life in keeping with those teachings. Believing in heaven and hell, he felt that people had the ability to choose between the two for where to spend eternity: "He [God] built heaven and hell and gives us strength to go to either one. . . . We got to meet Jesus someday and we need to be ready. Live right, because you can die before you can say, 'Lord, have mercy!' There's nothing on this earth you can get and take with you except religion. If you die a sinner, you're just a sinner." DeFord always tried to "live right" and do what he thought God wanted him to do. He didn't curse, smoke, drink any alcoholic beverages, or have any of a variety of other such habits that many men and women fall victim to. In his dealings with other people, he tried to live by the Golden Rule. "Money and clothes won't take you to heaven," he pointed out. "It's what's under them clothes that matters."

Reflecting his religious background, DeFord had clear-cut ideas and views on many of the major issues of the day. For example, during one of the critical energy shortages of the late 1970s, he expressed what he would have done if he were in charge of leading the country: "The Bible tells you everything you need to know. It tells of droughts, famines, and all. But we don't prepare. If I was president, we wouldn't have no shortages. I'd build big reservoirs for fuel and other things. I'd see that old things was fixed up instead of tearing them down."

He supported most of the existing government social welfare programs to help the old, the handicapped, and the poor, but he claimed they didn't always accomplish what they were intended to do. Some of the programs seem to penalize people who want to work full- or part-time to try to improve their condition.

"That's not right," he stated emphatically. There were other programs he would have liked to see expanded. He thought the food-stamp program should be broadened to include essentials like soap and cleaning products as well as foodstuffs. The government should "encourage people to keep themselves clean," he said.

DeFord thought some government programs were completely wasteful. He particularly opposed the money spent "on going to the moon." "If God wanted us up there, he'd have put us up there in the first place," he stated firmly. He felt strongly that our money should be spent on "taking care of people here on earth." Moreover, he wondered if these efforts were not creating other problems for the environment. As he explained, "every time they fool around with the moon, the weather gets strange." On crime, he was eager to see criminals punished for their wrongdoings, but he did not favor capital punishment under any conditions. "The Bible tells us not to kill one another," he pointed out.

One problem DeFord saw with the contemporary world was that people didn't love each other enough. Typically, he proposed how things should be by using an analogy with nature: "If we all loved one another like Bermuda grass sticks to the ground, we'd all go to the Kingdom of Heaven. You know how it holds in there and comes up thicker every year. It grows everywhere."

When the going got rough, he didn't hesitate to turn to the Lord in prayer, always finding help and consolation. "We need to ask God to help us through our troubles. You know, prayer is one telephone that will always work." The Lord "speaks" to us in a variety of ways, DeFord claimed, through many moral lessons or messages in nature and the simple things in life: "Everything has sense to it if we can just figure it out. God didn't put everything in the Bible. He expected us to figure some of it out by ourselves."

"Sometimes God reminds us to be humble and put our faith in Him," DeFord said. He pointed out the example of the *Titanic*, the greatest luxury ship ever made. It was supposed to be "unsinkable," but it sank with a great loss of life on April 14, 1912, a tragedy that made a big impression on DeFord, who was just a boy at the time. "It shows us that nothing man makes is above God," he said. His mother frequently sang a song about the sinking of the Titanic. "That's how come I knew so much about it," he said. "She sung it all the time." That song was probably similar to "Down with the Old Canoe," recorded by the Dixon Brothers from Darlington County, South Carolina. According to them, the Titanic was cut down in its pride by an iceberg because it was built by people and not by God. The message was clear: people should always be prepared to die, because no one knows when Christ will take them.

DeFord was not baptised until he joined the Greater Bethel African Methodist Episcopal (AME) Church in Nashville as an adult, but his religious convictions go back many years to his childhood. His foster mother was a devout Christian. Her influence on him as a young boy was particularly strong in this regard, as in so many others. She regularly took him with her to the Methodist Church she attended every Sunday and tried to teach him right from wrong.

A very strict Christian, she did not approve of certain types of dancing or music. However, she did enjoy hearing and singing religious songs. One of her favorites was "When the Saints Go Marching In," and while she would reprimand DeFord for playing the blues, especially on Sunday, she listened attentively whenever he played "The Saints" or other religious tunes on his harmonica.

DeFord experimented some as a child with dancing (tap dancing, buck dancing, the tango, and others). He was very quick to pick up the movements and learned all the new styles of the period. However, his "dancing career" came to a screeching halt when he was "eleven or twelve years old." He had been dancing the "Sally Long," a new tango. (DeFord says the full title was "Sally Long and Her Drop Stitch Stocking Was a Horrible Skirt.") His mother saw him doing it. She didn't like the motions, which she considered vulgar. "That was the only time Momma ever whipped me," DeFord said. "I could've been a good dancer, but after that, I put dancing down." As he saw it,

> I got a whipping over what Elvis Presley got rich on. He played "Black folks' songs," the same things we'd heard and known for years. He learned things from us. That's the way we sung from the beginning. Everything he played was in the Black style. He could make any kind of motion he wanted to, and they wouldn't say nothing to him.

As a child DeFord intended to become a minister of the gospel. He was even nicknamed "Preacher" at one time because of this. Although he later concluded that God did not want him to preach, he always believed that God was directing his life. DeFord didn't think it was just chance that made him a great harmonica player; he was convinced that it was God's will. His having been afflicted with polio at an early age and having been sickly as a child were parts of God's plan for him: "My condition made me develop my talent rather than wasting my time playing ball like more healthy children would have done."

Bailey on the balcony of his apartment, with his harmonica.
Photograph by Clark Thomas.

Bailey playing his guitar in his apartment in Edgehill.
Photograph by Dennis Wile.

God made him the way he was, he believed, and that "way" was musical through and through. His style came naturally; he seemed uniquely endowed to specialize on the harp:

My mouth is just like a mold for a harp. I can turn them sounds just like I want. If I don't blow my harp, I hurt. God put that on me to make me play. He wanted me to use my talent.

He made me want water. I'd drink water. That wouldn't satisfy it, though. But I'd play the harp and that feeling would go away. That's the way God would tell me to play my harp. That happened every day. All my life. I had to keep playing the harp, just like I had to keep drinking water.

If I was in a place where I couldn't play, He showed me how to stop the pain by moving my mouth like I was playing.

DeFord said God was clearly responsible for what he accomplished: "God gave me my talent, and He plays through me. I can be playing and notes will just come from nowhere that I never heard before. God taught me." Any praise for his skill should be to God, not to himself. "It ain't me, it's God in me," DeFord proclaimed. "His strength is too powerful for me to explain it."

In short, DeFord believed that God gave him the ability to play a harp, set the stage for him to develop his skills with the instrument, and encouraged and directed him in playing it. Much of this is summed up in a composition DeFord created in July 1974, when he was seriously ill in a Nashville hospital. It was a simple prayer, which he performed to his guitar accompaniment and played for friends later that fall when he was back on his feet and back home.

A Prayer

Sometime in the morning,
I don't know what to do,
And I lay down at night,
And I talk to the Good Lord,
Who's watching over me.
He's been watching over me
Many a year.

I don't know:
Sometime I don't know what to do,
You know, God,
I can't pray enough,
So I wake up in the morning,
I see the rising sun,
You let me walk,
Without somebody leading me,
Nobody but You.

Sometime I'm up and down the street,
I think I'm by myself,
I'm not never by myself,
The Good Lord's with me all the time,
But you don't want to see Him,
Oh, Lord, oh,
I wonder,
What's going to come of me someday,
I wouldn't mind dying,
But we got to die by ourself,
You got to walk that lonesome road,
One day by yourself,
You must think now,
About that.
I woke up one morning,
With the Good Lord on my mind,
I began to start talking.
Amen.

14

"Just Playing to Four Walls and to God"

By the 1960s, Nashville's music scene was exploding on two fronts. Country music was becoming increasingly slick and sophisticated, and the conglomeration of offices and studios that would become Music Row was developing along Fifteenth and Sixteenth avenues. Country songwriters like Willie Nelson, Tom T. Hall, and Mel Tillis were starting to arrive in town, sensing that careers could be found in the new industry. On the Opry, the cast that was known to DeFord and "Judge" George D. Hay was slowly fading away. Dr. Humphrey Bate had died in 1936, and the veteran stringbands that he had helped inspire were pretty much restricted to playing for Opry square-dance troupes and being combined or phased out. Roy Acuff, the McGee Brothers, and Bill Monroe were still there; people like Herman Crook, Jimmie Riddle, and Onie Wheeler kept the sound of the harmonica alive. But increasingly, as DeFord listened to the Saturday night broadcasts, he heard less and less of what he liked, and more and more new names who didn't know much about the Opry's history or its pioneers like DeFord Bailey.

There was another type of Nashville music emerging during this time, though, one not nearly as slick as the modern Opry, and much more in touch with its roots. This was soul music, which for a time in the 1960s threatened to make Nashville a major Black music center. In the late 1940s, WSM rival WLAC had become a nationwide forum for rhythm & blues records, and in the 1950s Nashville could boast of a number of independent record companies that featured Black music: Excello, Nashboro, Tennessee, and Bullet. By the 1960s, a second generation of record companies emerged, including such labels as Sound

Stage 7, SSS International, Dial, and Silver Fox. Along Jefferson Street in north-west Nashville, clubs rang with the sounds of exciting house bands featuring musicians like Jimmy Church, Gorgeous George, Ironing Board Sam, Earl Gaines, and Johnny Sneed. DeFord's son, DeFord Junior, had become a fine bass guitar player, and with his own son, DeFord III, who played drums, was part of this heady scene. Through him, DeFord himself became slightly involved as well.

One of the fruits of the Nashville soul scene was a syndicated television show called *Night Train* that ran from 1964 to 1967. Produced by broadcaster Noble Blackwell, "the host with the most," the show featured nationally known acts like Gladys Knight & the Pips as well as a wealth of local talent. It was taped on Tuesday nights at WLAC's old studios in the downtown Life & Casualty tower. DeFord Junior began to appear regularly on the show, working with a young guitar player who would shortly leave Nashville for the West Coast and gain fame as Jimi Hendrix. Hendrix was the acoustic and electric guitar player for Junior's band, which played at a club called the Jolly Roger in the Printer's Alley section of Nashville. Hendrix, at that time a conservative and quite religious young man, was fascinated with Junior's bass style, and later, after he gained fame, asked Junior to come to England with him. While in Music City, Hendrix became quite close to the Bailey family, often eating with them and visiting with DeFord Senior when the family got together. Though these two giants of Black American music—sepa-rated by generations yet linked by a love of the blues—never performed publicly together, they did visit and talk, and certainly Junior's association with Hendrix carried the Bailey tradition forward into a new generation of Black music.

Partly to help his son's career, and partly because he was an old friend and distant relative to the WLAC program manager, Clarence Gilchrist, DeFord agreed to make a few appearances on *Night Train*. The show, which aired at midnight on Saturdays, appealed largely to a Black audience—one of the few times in his career that DeFord had found himself in such a venue. Among the pieces he performed were, quite naturally, his train songs; in fact, Junior remembers that the *Night Train* producers were so fond of his father's performances that they often replayed them on tape giving viewers the impression that he was on the show more than he in fact was. Undeniably, though, he played a small but significant part in the show's success.

DeFord also appeared with his son and Junior's band at a handful of concerts. These were free park concerts organized by the Nashville Metro Parks and Recreation Department; DeFord appeared at the request of his son and grandson to help promote their careers. He took much interest in the musical talent of his

DeFord Bailey Jr., left, with two members of his band.
Photograph by John C. Streator Jr. Courtesy of DeFord Bailey Jr.

fifteen grandchildren and encourage them in whatever musical activity appealed to them. Granddaughter Jacquenette marched with the Tennessee State University Band while Dezoral Yvette sang with the TSU choir. Grandson Joseph became a minister of music at a local church while several others played in Nashville bands. DeFord was proud of them all, but took particular pride in the fact that DeFord III and Hershel performed overseas, something he never did himself. A third type of music sweeping through America—and through Nashville—during the 1960s was the so-called "folk revival." While it enriched fresh-faced young coffeehouse favorites like the Kingston Trio and Joan Baez, it also began to attract attention to some of the older genuine traditional singers, many of whom had drifted into obscurity or retirement. As young fans learned about some of the greats who had been radio and record stars in the 1920s and 1930s, they began to search them out. They were delighted to find that a number of the pioneers of the Grand Ole Opry —like Arthur Smith, the McGee Brothers, and Stringbean—were still performing as well as ever. And it was not long before their trail led to DeFord Bailey as well.

Vanderbilt University, in fact, had been placed in a curious position by the folk revival. National campus favorites, including the Kingston Trio, were booked on campus and presented in its church-like Neely Auditorium. But there was also a triumphant (and recorded for album release) appearance by Lester Flatt and Earl Scruggs—bluegrass stars and mainstays of a local music that Vanderbilt had studiously shunned for many years. The first Vanderbilt Folk Festival, in the spring of 1963, included bluegrass but not mainstream country performers. Among other ironies, it saw the English banjoist Barry Murphy playing Appalachian tunes, and the native Middle Tennessean Dick Hulan singing a medieval English ballad to his own lute accompaniment.

By the mid-1960s, Hulan had moved to Washington, D.C., where he became active in the Folklore Society of Greater Washington. One of the society's projects at the time was to locate and interview people who had performed on the Opry in its early years. DeFord Bailey's name, complete with the address of his shoeshine parlor (1145 Twelfth Avenue South), headed their list. Thus when Hulan found himself returning to graduate school at Vanderbilt in the fall of 1966, he soon looked DeFord up. By coincidence, about this time he was hired by the Nashville Presbytery to be manager of the Marketplace, a club located over a tailor's shop on West End Avenue. Opened in November 1966, it was the closest thing to a folk-music club Nashville had. One of the first scheduled performers Hulan booked was DeFord Bailey. The audiences were both youthful and racially mixed, and DeFord was an instant success; he returned to play several times over the following months. He also established friendships with some of the volunteers and patrons at the Marketplace, especially the Bill Myerses, the Archie Allens, the Dick Hulans, and the Barry Murphys.

Ordinarily Hulan drove DeFord to and from the coffeehouse and acted as emcee for his set. He would show up at DeFord's house a few minutes early to allow time for DeFord to dictate a list of pieces he intended to play that evening. The harmonica player was still shy about speaking on stage but wanted his numbers announced, just as they had been on the Opry; he also wanted to limit the length of time he had to spend on his feet. Tapes preserved two of these

Bailey playing his banjo, probably at a coffeehouse, in the late 1960s. Photograph given to Morton by Bailey for use in biography.

concerts and reveal an interesting selection of tunes—tunes that might at least give some hint of what DeFord considered his "core repertoire" at that time. In the concert of June 1967, for instance, he began with his "Fox Chase" and then moved on to a version of "John Henry," played in "the old-time way, the way his grandfather played it." Next came "It Ain't Gonna Rain No Mo'" another favorite from the distant past that he had never recorded, and then a piece called "Bunch of Blues." This showed up on several concerts during the 1960s, and it too had not been previously recorded by him; it was a fast, jazzy number that resembled in some ways the old hillbilly song "You Ain't Talking to Me." The short concert—it ran little more than fifteen minutes—concluded with "Pan American" and "Lost John." At one point, Hulan commented to the audience, "If Bobby Dylan could practice another forty-five years, he'd be able to do that."

The atmosphere of the Marketplace soon became noted for its free exchange of opinion—lectures and speeches were as common as music—and it was soon attracting the most vocal civil rights and antiwar activists in the Nashville region. Often these included representatives of organizations like SCLC, SNCC, and SSOC; in late 1966, this latter group (the Southern Student Organizing Committee) brought to town its touring "Southern Music Festival." The festival was held in Neely Auditorium at Vanderbilt, with DeFord as an invited guest. On that show, he played several harmonica numbers and then took up his banjo, which had just been renovated by Barry Murphy and still bore the red ribbon indicating that the repair job was a gift. With it DeFord embarked on a rousing version of "Lost John." It was memorable. Playing his instrument left-handed (and upside down), DeFord showed off his old drop-thumb clawhammer style; he sang, crowed, hollered, and at times seemed to be doing an imitation of Uncle Dave Macon. Folk music great Pete Seeger, who was present to do a banjo workshop for the event, and who himself was a devotee of Uncle Dave, was so impressed that he got up at one point and walked across the stage, leaning closer to see what DeFord was doing with his fingering. Tapes of this concert also exist and show that DeFord was still a formidable banjoist, even though he had not played much in recent years.

This circle of friends continued to try to stimulate interest in DeFord's career. Bill Myers was a commercial artist and did some excellent sketches of DeFord performing at the Marketplace; one of these appeared in the Nashville *Tennessean* of January 5, 1974, when it won a gold medal in the annual competition of the Art Directors Club of Nashville. Archie Allen, a civil rights activist who lived near DeFord, promoted him, as well as other musicians like Len Chandler and John Hartford, whose style and repertoire were suitable to the coffeehouse scene. Hartford, who later became a leading bluegrass star best known for his famous song "Gentle on My Mind," remembers that DeFord "opened" for him at one of his first club dates in Nashville in 1967, and that among the audience that night were members of the folk-rock group the Byrds. Allen had arranged both dates, for Hartford and Bailey. Allen moved to Atlanta in 1971 but always visited DeFord when he returned to Nashville; once he delighted the harmonica player by presenting him with a $5 bill made into a bow tie.

Many of the veteran musicians rediscovered by the folk revival found themselves described as "folk" or "traditional," though for generations they had considered themselves "country" musicians and thought of themselves as professionals. Some, like the McGee Brothers, had always been close to their roots and were perfectly happy to call themselves folk musicians; others, like ex-Skillet Licker fiddler Clayton McMichen, had problems with the idea. DeFord had always loved, respected, and acknowledged his folk music roots— he was especially anxious to point out the importance of Black stringband music—but he had also struggled hard to win respect as a professional musician, and during his glory years on the Opry he wore his WSM pin proudly and felt part of an elite corps. The pros were the ones up on the stage or in front of the radio microphones; the amateurs were the "folk" who played at local dances and on front porches.

Now DeFord was finding himself being described as "folk." Dick Hulan, by now a young folklore scholar who taught summer seminars in the subject at Vanderbilt, took his students to visit and interview DeFord and presented him as a "folk" musician at several Nashville clubs and coffeehouses. The prestigious Newport Folk Festival, the nation's biggest and best known, invited him to come, but it was a long way to Rhode Island, and DeFord turned them down. The leading state folk festival, the annual fiddling contest held at Clarksville, Tennessee, asked DeFord to be a guest of honor in the 1970s, but he declined the invitation.

During this time, there were a number of attempts to get DeFord into the recording studio. Fans had heard at concerts how well DeFord could still play the harmonica and had heard numerous tunes that he had never recorded on the old 78s, which were by now long out of print. They had also heard DeFord play guitar and banjo and sing, none of which had been preserved on records at all. One person who tried was Mike Weesner, a young independent producer who had good ties with major labels in Nashville. In 1967, Weesner had run across Cortelia Clark, a blind street singer, and persuaded RCA Victor to record him; the resulting album was *Blues in the Street,* which won a Grammy in 1967 for Best Folk Album (though it never sold many copies). Weesner thought an album by DeFord would be a natural follow-up, and often visited the shoeshine stand to talk about it—all to no avail. At one point Weesner had gotten close enough to an agreement that he had arranged a ride for DeFord to come to the recording studio, but things fell through at the last minute. "It would have been another Grammy," he lamented. In the late 1960s, the man who was recognized as perhaps the country's leading folksinger, Pete Seeger, came to Nashville to perform on *The Johnny Cash Show*. Not having known that Bailey was still alive, Seeger was eager to record him. Pete invited DeFord to join him on the album that eventually became *Pete Seeger Young vs. Old*. Columbia Records offered Bailey an impressive flat fee, plus a percentage of the royalties; this too he turned down. Later, Nashville session

James Talley, left, Bailey, and David Morton standing on the balcony of Bailey's apartment. Photograph by Clark Thomas.

man and the town's leading country harmonica player, Charlie McCoy, tried to get DeFord to play on one of his albums, with similar results.

About 1970, DeFord became friends with James Talley, a young singer and songwriter from Oklahoma who had spent a number of years in the Southwest as a welfare worker. By the mid-1970s, Talley's musical career was starting to take off; he was signed by Capitol for a series of well-received albums, many derived from his fondness for early country music and blues. His interest in DeFord dated from when he was working in the health department in Nashville and was introduced to DeFord by some Black friends. At that time, Talley recalls, DeFord was still reticent around people he didn't know but was also basically "lonesome" and had a love of performing that often overcame his suspicions.

A musician himself, Talley was impressed with what DeFord could accomplish technically, especially "his ability to play rhythm and melody at the same time. He played in a straight harp way, not what so many other bluesmen do in cross-harp style. He could do things with the harmonica that were just incredible. The closest person today who can do this is [guitarist and singer] Doc Watson." Talley used his contacts in the industry to try to interest other labels in recording DeFord, and at one time even wrote to John Hammond Sr., the veteran Columbia Records New York A&R man who had been responsible for the careers of major artists from Billie Holiday to Bob Dylan. None of this panned out, however, and Talley began to seriously worry that DeFord might not get to record any of his later music, that all the wonderful sounds and songs would simply be lost with his death.

After I became friends with DeFord in 1973, he began to call me his "manager" and wanted me to handle all arrangements for the few public appearances he made in later life. Many of these were local, low-key affairs, with audiences composed of casual fans and friends rather than folk music buffs or blues enthusiasts. In 1974, for instance, I persuaded him to perform at two functions held by the Metro Development and Housing Agency, the organization that operated the high-rise where Bailey lived. One was a gathering of agency employees, the other an audience of elderly residents. Playing harp, guitar, and banjo, he was a big hit with both groups.

He also played a few private parties. One was for the manager of Opryland, the giant amusement park that had been built next to the new Grand Ole Opry House in northeast Nashville. DeFord's son had worked at Opryland that summer and had promised to get his "daddy" to play at the boss's party; fortunately for him, his "daddy" agreed. Another time, I arranged for DeFord to perform at a Christmas party for the employees of the Nashville Sash & Door Company, at

Bailey performing at the WSM Grand Ole Opry with Minnie Pearl and Roy Acuff looking on. WSM photograph by Les Leverett.

the home of the owner, Sidney McAlister. A different sort of party was one hosted by a Vanderbilt graduate student, Marshall Fallwell, to celebrate completing his Ph.D. in English. Fallwell had known DeFord for four years; he often brought others by the apartment to meet him, usually giving DeFord $10 to $20 when he did. At one time Fallwell tried to get DeFord to go over to Memphis and play, but was unsuccessful.

Certainly the most important performances I arranged during these later years were a series of guest appearances on the Grand Ole Opry itself. The first was at the initial "Old Timers' Night" on February 23, 1974; the second was on December 14, 1974, in honor of DeFord's seventy-fifth birthday; the third was in 1975 at another "Old Timers' Night"; and the fourth came in 1982. WSM executive Jud Collins and I got the idea for the "Old Timers' Night" during an interview I was conducting with him about DeFord. "I wonder just what it would take to get DeFord back on the Opry stage," Collins mused. Soon plans for the show were underway, expanded to include a homecoming program for various older Opry stars that had drifted into retirement, but principally as a means to get the legend-ary "Harmonica Wizard" back on the Opry stage.

Though DeFord had not been an official Opry guest since his firing in 1941, he had made occasional appearances on the show in the 1940s and 1950s. For the most part, these were situations where an Opry star like Bill Monroe would come to DeFord and pay him out of his own pocket to be a guest on that star's segment of the Opry broadcast on a given evening. Even these incidents had become rare, though, and DeFord turned down offer after offer. By 1974, he had not been on the Opry stage in over a decade. Also, the show was to be one of the last held at the old Ryman Auditorium, the classic tabernacle that had housed the Opry for some thirty-odd years. Though it was the Opry house of Hank Williams, Red Foley, Rod Brasfield, and others, it was not really the Opry house DeFord knew; when he had left in 1941, the Opry was still being held in the War Memorial Auditorium on Capitol Hill in Nashville.

Nevertheless, there was plenty of drama when DeFord stepped out on the Opry stage. The show also included such veterans as Clyde Moody, Zeke Clements, Uncle Dave Macon's old sidekick Sid Harkreader, Dr. Humphrey Bate's daughter Alcyone Bate Beasley, Kirk McGee & the Fruit Jar Drinkers, and the team of Pee Wee King and Redd Stewart, composers of "The Tennessee Waltz." Roy Acuff and Minnie Pearl hosted the segment featuring the old-timers, and as it started, current members of the Opry cast stopped their gossiping backstage and crowded up to the wings to see some of the living legends they had heard so much about. After Acuff played a suitably old-time song, "Whoa, Mule," Pee Wee King took the stage with his accordion and did some of his trademark songs. Next came Sid Harkreader, fiddling his "Mocking Bird Breakdown" and the Uncle Dave Macon favorite "How Beautiful Heaven Must Be." Acuff then introduced DeFord, and as Minnie Pearl stood by and clapped, DeFord went into his "Pan American." After prolonged applause, he did the "Fox Chase," his other trademark piece. Backstage

Howard "Howdy" Forrester, a member of Roy Acuff's band, with Bailey backstage at the new Opry House in Opryland. WSM photograph by Les Leverett.

Roy Acuff with Bailey backstage at the Opry's "Old Timers' Night" at the Ryman.
WSM photograph by Les Leverett.

there were congratulations and handshakes, and afterwards DeFord went to an
informal gathering at my home, where he entertained friends with some of the
tunes he had not played on the show that night.

The second of the appearances was in actuality even more dramatic. It occurred
on December 14, 1974, about nine months after the Opry had moved from the
Ryman to the new five-thousand-seat, state-of-the-art Opry house out near the
Opryland amusement park. DeFord, like many of the older performers who had
been with the show since its days of drafty tents and straw-covered floors, was
impressed with the huge glittering hall that was now home for the Opry.

For weeks the publicity had geared up for the event, and local news stories
bore titles like "DeFord Bailey Comes Home to the Opry" (Nashville *Tennessean,*
December 16, 1974). Bailey appeared on Roy Acuff's segment of the show. Acuff
introduced him by saying:

I owe a whole lot to the gentleman I'm going to introduce. To some of you, he will be a complete stranger, but you who have listened to the Grand Ole Opry many years back will remember him, and remember that he was one of the first people to come on the Grand Ole Opry. . . . When he starts playing, I won't have to tell you that he is the man who introduced this type of music to the Grand Ole Opry. I've got some good ones with me, Onie Wheeler and Jimmie Riddle, fine harmonica players, but when it comes to where they learned it, this was one of the teachers.

Once again, DeFord Bailey walked out onto an Opry stage, though one bigger and brighter than he had ever seen. He and Acuff reminisced briefly about their old days together, back when Bailey was used to lure the crowds to see a then-unknown Roy Acuff, and when they spent hours together driving miles on narrow, winding, two-lane roads. Acuff remembered, "A many a night you slept on my shoulder, and many a night I slept on yours." "That's right," replied DeFord. Acuff then asked him to start off with the "Pan American," and DeFord launched into his famous whistle drone. After the first few bars, the audience began applauding; even the ones who had never seen or heard DeFord sensed that here was something special. Next, Acuff asked Bailey if he would like to play "Lost John," but DeFord had plans of his own; he wanted, he said, to play the one he won his first contest with, on WDAD back in 1925, "It Ain't Gonna Rain No Mo'." Acuff then asked him how his children were; there were three children, Bailey replied, and fifteen grandchildren, and four great-grandchildren. After another round of applause, he launched into his trademark song, "The Fox Chase." Then it was over; his second comeback had lasted about ten minutes, but it was the high point of the night.

Backstage, amidst the cowboy hats and spangled suits of a new generation of Opry members, were some old familiar faces that DeFord remembered. There was Alcyone Bate Beasley, whose father had first taken DeFord to WSM and who later said that he was "the dangdest harmonica player who ever lived." There were Sam and Kirk McGee, who toured with him for years with Uncle Dave Macon; there were Herman and Lewis Crook, of the Crook Brothers Band, who had kept the harmonica sound alive on the show. Bill Monroe, the "man who liked Oldsmobiles," was off touring in Japan. Along with congratulations from these old friends, veteran Opry staffers, newspaper reporters, and young enthusiasts who had heard DeFord prove that he was still as good as everybody said he was, there was a birthday cake in honor of DeFord's seventy-fifth birthday. All in all it was a good night, and DeFord was glad he had let me talk him into coming.

Cake given to Bailey on his seventy-fifth birthday by Herman Crook, Alcyone Bate Beasley, Roy Acuff, and members of Acuff's band. WSM photograph by Les Leverett.

In the meantime, offers continued to pour in, and fans continued to make pilgrimages to see him. The manager in his high-rise began to get a steady stream of calls from people who had heard about him or wanted to interview him or engage him for some performance or another. Visitors included Bill Malone, author of *Country Music, USA,* the standard history of the genre, and Hans Zeiman, the German blues scholar who was now cultural editor of *Stern.* Joe Wilson, who had known DeFord in the 1950s, invited the musician to the prestigious National Folk Festival in Washington—an offer DeFord politely refused. He turned down $2,500 to play three tunes and appear in the 1975 Burt Reynolds film *W. W. and the Dixie Dancekings;* the part then went to Memphis bluesman Furry Lewis, though it seemed written for DeFord. Magazine writers, television talk show hosts, newspaper reporters, promoters of various sorts—all made their way to DeFord's high-rise, and all went away empty-handed.

DeFord knew that many of these offers could have been stepping stones to a comeback and revival of his career. "A whole lot of my talent went down the drain," he said, reflecting over the forty-year period, from 1941 to 1982, when he did not regularly perform. There were a number of reasons why he passed up so many opportunities. He had learned from experience just what he was worth as a performer, and didn't think it unreasonable to turn down offers that fell short of this mark. "I never was a money hound, and I never wanted nothing big," he explained, but at the same time he didn't need to perform just for the recognition and acclaim. "That name ain't enough. When I go in a store, I gotta have some money."

On one occasion, he was approached by a young European filmmaker doing a documentary on country music for educational television in Europe. He told DeFord he was working on a shoestring budget, and could not afford to pay him more than $50 to $100 for appearing in it. DeFord politely declined. Later he told me that, if the man could afford to come all the way to the United States to film his movie, he had to have enough money to pay adequately: "He didn't walk across that ocean, did he? He had to pay to get over here and pay for a place to stay. He can afford to pay me."

Similarly, he turned down the Opry's request for him to appear on their later Old Timers' Reunion shows in 1976 and 1977. He would have received the Opry's standard pay of $50 a show—the pay every performer got, regardless of rank. DeFord argued: "They don't want to pay me. They just want to take my picture. Like their monkey. Well, I've had enough of that. If they would treat me right, I'd go back in a minute."

In fact, DeFord didn't feel compelled to perform as he once had. He no longer had a family to support; he and his wife had been divorced for several years, and all his children were grown and on their own. He had no reason to prove himself to anyone. He certainly didn't owe the Opry any favors. He also knew he was getting older, and he simply didn't have the energy to travel long distances or be away from home for long periods. If he was going to perform anywhere in public, he expected adequate compensation. "If I go on that stage, pay me just like the top man," he said. "If you can't do that, I'll just play to these four walls and to God. . . . I don't want to be over nobody, nor under nobody. I just want to be in there with 'em. I don't want to get in front. I'm just like a hound dog. I just want to run along with 'em. That's all." DeFord's reaction to an offer from ABC television during this time illustrates this attitude. The network was filming a special on country music at the Opry, and they wanted DeFord. He was offered $400, the same amount being paid to the regular Opry performers on the program. It was far less, though, than what they were paying superstar Johnny Cash, who was heading up the show. DeFord insisted he would perform only if he were paid as much as anyone else on the show, including Cash, whatever that amount was. Even a personal plea from his old friend Roy Acuff did not budge him, and the show went on without him.

Another reason he rejected so many offers was that he was wary, even suspicious, of being cheated or used for someone else's gain. He had seen many a con artist or fast-talking promoter in his day. "This world is crooked as a barrel of snakes," he once said. "You don't know who you can trust."

Some of "the white folks" who came to him with proposals for festivals, television shows, and concerts interpreted his negative response as racial prejudice. However, DeFord was just as cautious about Blacks who proposed various enterprises. Race actually had nothing to do with his reticence. He told me: "They say I don't like white people. They got that wrong. I'm just like white people. I just want my money. I don't hate the man. I just hate his ways. . . . I just want my money from Black or white. Like a union that goes on strike. I don't want more than everyone else, but I want the same as they got."

Friends think that part of this attitude came from DeFord never really having got over his crude dismissal from the Opry in 1941. There was a certain safety in avoiding recording sessions or public performances: if he didn't perform, he wouldn't be exploited. On the other hand, he lost invaluable opportunities—to make himself known to new fans in the 1970s and 1980s, and to preserve his rare repertoire. Only when I bought him a small cassette recorder and urged him to record himself in the privacy of his own room did he begin to preserve some of his tunes. Later he allowed me to make a series of better-quality tapes of some of his songs as a means of preserving his music through modern technology.

DeFord always claimed that, in the right situation and with the right money, he would play his heart out and show everyone that he was still the "humdinger" that he was in the 1920s. But the magic combination never took place. Still, he was satisfied with what he had accomplished and, in boastful moments, could even joke about his preeminence in the field:

I'm an old man now. But they never will get out of a harp what I can. They're just wasting their time trying to beat me on a harp. Ain't nobody ever set me down with no harp. Trying to beat me blowing is like trying to outrun a Greyhound bus! I got notes harder than Muhammad Ali can throw. I could throw some notes on him that would fair paralyze him!

And like a heavyweight champ, he could pick and choose his contenders; in the last ten years of his life, there were more important things than securing a reputation.

15

"You Have to Learn to Live with Old Age"

By 1971, the rough-and-tumble neighborhood of Edgehill, which DeFord had once known as "Rocktown," was becoming a more respectable Black neighborhood. Urban renewal had removed most of the truly run-down slum buildings and created wide streets, modern lighting, parks, and new or rehabilitated housing. The population had become increasingly stable and middle-class, and while crime and violence were still problems, they were no more so than in the neighboring white areas. DeFord was very much in the middle of these changes. By 1970, the Nashville Housing Authority had bought DeFord's old house and torn it down, and a year later it took over his shoeshine parlor at the corner of Edgehill and Twelfth; soon it was gone too, and DeFord found himself living in a federally subsidized high-rise for the elderly—located, ironically, just across the corner from where he had operated his shoeshine stand.

DeFord was at first unsettled by all the changes to his old neighborhood. "They're tearing everything down around here," he told a reporter in 1970. "That's what really hurts. When a man passes on and he's got a house, at least when he goes people can drive by and say, 'Right there, that's where DeFord lived, right there in that old house there.'" But he soon began to see the advantages of his high-rise apartment. Granted, it was small; it overflowed with the belongings he had collected through the years, and he had little room for overnight visits by family or friends. He could not keep dogs like he once had. But his rent was low (it was adjusted to his income), he had good neighbors, and the building was clean and well kept. He remembered having "stayed in some of the finest places, and in some of the worst—rats, bugs, and all that. . . . Where I live now is like a palace compared to some places I stayed." He especially liked the security of the

DeFord Bailey with his children Dezoral, Christine, and DeFord Jr., and David Morton, 1970s.

high-rise; there was a live-in maintenance staff, and the building was kept locked at night. The residents thus faced few of the problems of crime and vandalism that many elderly persons face in low-income neighborhoods.

In 1973, when I met DeFord, he was at a "low" period in his life. He had been forced to close his venerable shoeshine stand and was becoming more and more of a recluse in his apartment. He brooded about his life and career, feeling he had been cheated out of his proper due. Having little money, he could not afford to do many of the things he wanted to do. More than anything else, though, he was depressed because he was getting, as he described it, "hard of hearing," and the situation was getting worse. It was the ultimate nightmare for a musician. DeFord found he was having to play more loudly and with more bass if he wanted to really hear what he sounded like: "My ears and things, they getting away. You know, you got to hear yourself when you doing anything like that. Now, I don't listen like you listen. I listen with close hearing, I don't know what you call it, music listening. See, it don't sound to me like it sounds to you. I listen just enough to carry the tune. Just like a person is blind, he can go all over his house and find anything. That's how I blow this harp."

As DeFord and I became friends, I soon suggested the idea of a hearing aid. Bailey's first reaction was that it would be a waste of time, but eventually he agreed to go for an examination. An appointment for testing was made with a specialist at the Bill Wilkerson Speech and Hearing Clinic. To everyone's surprise,

David Morton holding microphone while Bailey plays banjo at a function held for employees of the Metropolitan Development and Housing Agency in Nashville. Photograph by Rayburn Ray. Courtesy of the Metropolitan Development and Housing Agency.

it turned out that much of the hearing problem was due to a buildup of wax in his ears. There was some need for a hearing aid, but DeFord seldom used it. The wax was removed, and his hearing dramatically improved. "Now I can hear a fly cough with the whooping cough," DeFord laughed.

Since hearing meant so much to a musician like DeFord, it was not surprising to find that his improvement caused a major change in his whole outlook on life. His general attitude became more positive; he began to dwell more in the present and to plan for the future rather than brood about the past. Now he could again enjoy his music and spend hours entertaining himself with it. He began to talk about more public appearances, and even about cutting an album. He began to enjoy life again—a fact that was commented on by several of his neighbors and family members. He began to accept his retirement more gracefully. "You have to learn to live with old age," he reminded a neighbor when she complained about not being able to drive her car anymore. "An old man can't do what he could do when he was twenty."

With few teeth and limited stamina, DeFord obviously couldn't play his harp the way he had when he was young. Knowing that, he didn't try to kid himself, but it didn't stop him from playing whenever he felt the urge. He simply adjusted his style to his limitations; he did not try to play continuously for long periods of time, but he played as often as he wanted, which was still usually several times a day. If he couldn't make a particular note, he found another to take its place: "My music today is like an old car. I can't get some of the parts for it no more. So I have to put in new parts. I do the same thing with my music."

His love of music remained as strong as ever. He liked to point out that it was as strong as an addiction to alcohol or drugs. "Music is like dope. I get just like a dope addict on music. I'm telling you the truth. But you can put them in an asylum and get it out of them. You can't get it out of me. I'm just as full of it as I can be. I can't help it. I can go to bed not thinking about music, and I'll wake up just full of it." When he was "full of it," DeFord was almost compelled to "make music." It was relief and satisfaction to play his harp—"I'd rather play than eat." When he got wound up in his music, he could easily miss a meal and not notice it.

Most of the time, however, DeFord was very conscious of his health. He knew that people his age were vulnerable to colds and viruses, and that an apartment house was an especially bad place to catch bugs. "When you get to be my age, you're just good fertilizer for any old germ," he said. In bad weather, he insisted on staying inside; "if that cold air hits us, it's like a weed getting wilted."

His daily routine was to get up early, take a bath, and shave. "Even the poorest person can afford some Ivory soap," he said. He also kept his apartment scrupulously neat, remembering his mother's dictum that "if a house is good enough to live in, it's good enough to keep clean." He always put on a clean white dress shirt, dress pants, and a tie of some sort. Then, with his apron over his clothes, he would cook himself breakfast, eat, and wash the dishes. Next, he did whatever chores needed doing. At some time during the morning, he would find some time to play his harp; he would occasionally "pick a little" on his guitar or banjo, but he had to have a dose of "that harp."

Noon brought a simple meal of meat and vegetables. He preferred the kind of plain southern food he grew up on: white beans, ham hock, turnip greens, and corn bread. He didn't like much dessert, but he would take a little egg custard if it was not too sweet. After eating and cleaning up, he would spend the rest of the afternoon with his "best friend," his harp. He liked to say that "a harp has been a mother and father to me" and once told a friend: "This harp has carried me places

Bailey with his gourd megaphone.
Photograph by David Morton.

money wouldn't start to . . . and brought me back. It's worth a million dollars just to have and play around on. . . . It's company to me."

Even after playing for over seventy-five years, DeFord was still learning about harps:

> I learn something new about a harp every day or two. You never learn everything about one. It's just like growing. . . . I still hit new notes. One'll pop up every now and then. There are so many sounds that come out of this harp. Every day I'm alive, I hear a different sound. I'll be playing along and a note'll rise up, and stay with me for a while, then die down. It just happens. I don't do it intentionally.

He was still willing to learn from other people, but didn't expect to really gain much that way.

> I was sitting here in this chair one night and got to thinking, well, I done made seventy-five years in music. . . . If they can find any more notes than

The metal megaphone Bailey had made, with his harmonica placed in it. Photograph by David Morton.

I done found, okay. I searched it real good, but I got sense enough to know there's some more that I ain't found. I know that much. Now if they can find it, okay. I'd just like to hear 'em. If they find something I ain't never done, if I like it, it's mine; if I don't, well. . . .

Once a day DeFord would go downstairs to the lobby to get his mail. Occasionally he would sit for a while and visit with other residents, though he stayed away from any formal group activities: "I never did mix with nobody. None of them boys around here. I never did run with 'em. Nothing. I never had but one buddy and me and him was pretty well alike. He [Willie Copeland] married my foster sister. He's dead now." DeFord did come to rely on one resident of the building, Mrs. Elnora Moore, a retired teacher. She helped him by reading his mail to him, writing letters for him, paying any bills that needed a check written. Mrs. Moore and some of his other neighbors would drop in during the day to see how DeFord was doing—joking with him, commenting on his clothes, talking about the weather. When the weather was bad, they talked on the phone.

Bailey with David Morton's oldest son, Wilson, in his lap.
Photograph by David Morton.

Supper was usually leftovers warmed up, and then it was time for more music. Occasionally, there was television, though only for the music; often he had the radio and television on at the same time, neither turned high. He usually listened to a local Black station, WVOL, or to one of the Nashville country music stations.

Sometimes company would come after supper, and that often meant an evening's good talking. Though he enjoyed friends, DeFord remained wary of persons he did not know. If he felt comfortable with visitors, he would invite them in and even entertain them with his music. He delighted in showing people different sounds on his harp, and he would often "get going" with his music before the evening was over. If someone came by that he did not know, or did not feel good about, he was invariably polite, would thank them for coming by, but leave them outside his apartment door. Never ugly or curt, he would tell them he had a manager, and ask them to call me.

Even though the apartment was small, visitors were always impressed with how much stuff was packed into it. "It looks like an antique shop, sure enough," DeFord would laugh. He had three wardrobes, a chest of drawers, a dresser, and a closet, all of which were packed to the brim. Things were even stored on top of or under the furniture. "You never know when something may come in handy," he

Bailey playing his banjo in his apartment. Photograph by Clark Thomas.

said; regardless of the kind of problem that presented itself, DeFord always had a tool or a part to fix it—though he might have to hunt a while for it.

Other items he kept were heirlooms, icons, unusual props—souvenirs of a rich and full life. There was his famous walking stick that folded out into a seat; it probably wouldn't support the full weight of an average man, but it was perfect for the ninety-eight-pound DeFord. He had a miner's lamp that he bought back in the 1930s on an Opry trip to Bluefield, West Virginia. Stuck away in a drawer was a "boot puller," a wooden handle with a metal hook made to help pull on boots. For over forty years, DeFord had used it to put on his pants, hooking it in one of the belt loops. Then there were three megaphones that he had used on stage to amplify his harp: one was store-bought, made of fancy painted metal; the second was made for him by a friend out of metal; and a third was an old gourd that DeFord had carved by hand.

He had all models and sizes of harmonicas, from one "as small as a June bug" to one "so big it would choke a horse." For years he had preferred a Hohner Marine Band, one of the best-known standard brands; in later years, though, he became a little disenchanted with the brand: "they don't make 'em like they used to. I used to buy 'em for a quarter and they'd play. Now you're lucky to ever find a

Bailey on the balcony of his apartment in Nashville. Photograph by David Morton.

good one. When I do find a good one, I usually have to rebuild it." He continued to prefer a "plain harp" to one with various gadgets on it. He explained, "Them gadgets are for people who don't really know how to play a harp."

The walls of the apartment contained a strange assortment of pictures, memorabilia, and other items. There were photos of himself as well as of friends and fellow performers like Alcyone Bate Beasley, Vito Pellettieri (the Opry music librarian), Sid Harkreader (the veteran fiddler who worked with Uncle Dave Macon), Roy Acuff, Herman Crook, Kirk McGee—and one photo of the entire Opry cast. There was also a large picture of Jesus on one wall, as well as prints of trains, animals, and musical instruments. A cow shoe hung from a hook in one corner. Two souvenirs from his Opry days were on the wall as well: the old cow horn he used to blow as part of his routine on the "Fox Chase," and an old bell he rang with his train songs.

Trains were everywhere. There were several small toy trains, a larger train, a flowerpot shaped like a train, and items relating to trains or train terminals. One large print he displayed showed Nashville's stately Union Station. Some of these were gifts from admiring fans or his children, and as he grew older and more feeble, and got out of his apartment less and less, they became more and more important to him.

Bailey in his favorite chair in his apartment with some of the photographs and memorabilia he kept on display. Photograph by Clark Thomas.

A great deal had been lost over the years. He had none of the original 78-rpm records he had made for Victor and Brunswick in the 1920s, nor the classic Victor phonograph with the large, fancy speaker that he had bought then. Three children and several moves had put an end to those. An old steamboat whistle Judge Hay had given him had also been lost. The whistle had been Hay's trademark on the air; Hay had used it to open and close all the Opry shows as well as to express particular approval when a "hot tune" had been played. "I heard that thing many a time after I played that train," Bailey remembered with pride.

In his later years, he considered moving in with relatives or possibly even marrying again; he realized that living alone had its drawbacks. As long as he remained basically healthy, he could take care of himself, but he wondered what would happen if he became sick or disabled. There were days when he didn't feel like cooking a full meal for himself, and his diet suffered accordingly. If he had had a wife, a younger woman not quite in the "run-down" condition he was in, he felt he would at least be able to depend on a good meal and have someone to look after him.

He dreaded especially the prospect of having to enter a nursing home. "Folks crowded six to a room with nothing to do except to die," was the way he described it. As it turned out, he remained in surprisingly good health until just a few weeks before his death. He had some "aches and pains," but was able to care for himself. He attributed this to the kind of life he had led: "Life is a funny thing. You can make yourself old or you can make yourself young. When you tear yourself up by drinking and carrying on, you are shortening your own life. I never did that, and now I can go to bed and sleep pretty good." Still, he knew death could not be too far ahead; he gave instructions to me and to his family as to the type of funeral arrangements he desired. He wanted the same funeral home that had handled both his foster mother's and his foster father's funerals to handle his.

He was not fearful of death. He believed strongly in an afterlife and fully expected to see Clark and Barbara Lou and his old friends in heaven. But he was fearful that history would misunderstand him. He wanted people to know the kind of person he was and what had happened to him. He wanted everybody, "white and Black, to know the truth." This was the main reason DeFord wanted this book written. As he explained to me when he asked me to write this biography:

> I want you to tell the world about this Black man. He ain't no fool. Just let people know what I am. . . .
>
> I take the bitter with the sweet. Every day is Sunday with me. I'm happy-go-lucky.
>
> Amen!

Appendix

Musical Selections Performed by DeFord Bailey

"Alberta, Don't Grieve about a Dime"

"Alcoholic Blues"

"Amazing Grace"

"Black Man Blues" (on guitar)

"Bunch of Blues"

"Bye Bye Blackbird"

"Casey Jones"

"Comin' 'Round the Mountain"
   (on harp and banjo)

"Cow Cow Blues"

"Cry Holy unto the Lord"

"Davidson County Blues"

"Dixie Flyer Blues"

"Early in the Morning"

"Evening Prayer Blues"

"Every Time I Feel the Spirit"

"Fox Chase"

"Get Out and Get under the Moon"

"Gonna Eat at the Welcome Table Some
   of These Days"

"Good News"

"Gotta See Mama Every Night"

"Greyhound Blues" (on guitar)

"Guitar Blues" (on guitar)

"Has the Cat Got the Whoopin' Cough
   and the Dog Got the Measles"

"Hesitation Mama"

"Howling Blues" (on guitar)

"Ice Water Blues"

"I'll Fly Away"

"In the Evening"

"In the Sweet Bye and Bye"

"It Ain't Gonna Rain No Mo'"

"John Henry"

"Kansas City Blues" (I'm Going to
   Kansas City") (on harp and guitar)

"Little Sallie Gooden"

"Lost John" (on harp and banjo)

"Muscle Shoals Blues"

"My Blue Heaven" (DeFord wanted to
   play on the air, but Judge Hay
   wouldn't let him)

"Nashville Blues"

"Nice Like That"

"Old Hen Cackle"

"Old Joe Clark"

"Old Time Religion"

"Over in the Glory Land"

"Pan American Blues"

"A Prayer" (on guitar)

"Rattlesnake Blues" (played on guitar
   and harp)

"Sally Long"

"Sally Sittin' in a Saucer"

"Shake That Thing"

"Shoe Shine Boy Blues"

"Sitting on Top of the World"

"Soup Cow, Come Get Your Nubbins,
      Eat That One Up and Come Get
      Another One"

"Sweet Marie"

"Swing Low, Sweet Chariot"

"Up Country Blues"

"Way Down upon the Swanee River"

"When the Saints Go Marching In"

"Whoa, Mule, Whoa"

"Wood Street Blues"

"The Worry Blues" (on guitar)

"Yes, Sir, That's My Baby"

Sources

Interviews by David Morton

Interviews with DeFord Bailey in his Apartment in Nashville

Tape Number	Date	Length (in Minutes)	Contents
1	October 19, 1973	90	Interview
2	October 30, 1973	90	Songs, conversation
3	October 30, 1973	60	Songs, conversation
4A	October 30, 1973	30	Songs, conversation
4B	November 25, 1973	30	Songs, conversation
5	November 4, 1973	90	Songs, conversation
6	November 4, 1973	90	Songs, conversation
7	November 11, 1973	90	Songs, conversation
8	November 17, 1973	90	Songs, conversation
9A	November 30, 1973	45	Guitar and harp
9B	December 2, 1973	45	Guitar and harp
10	December 2, 1973	60	Conversation, tunes
11	December 15, 1973	60	Songs
12A	December 12, 1973	45	Conversation, guitar, harp
12B	January 2, 1974	45	Conversation, tunes
13	January 2, 1974	120	Guitar, harp
14	January 1974	90	Conversation, guitar
15	January 1974	60	Conversation, tunes
16	February 23, 1974	90	Informal concert
17	March 30, 1974	90	Open house
18	Undated	45	Conversation, banjo, guitar
19	October 1974	60	Four tunes
20	November 4, 1974	60	Conversation, tunes
21	January 1975	90	Conversation
22	October 17, 1976	60	Conversation

23	February 1978	60	Conversation
24	February 1978	60	Conversation
25	1982	30	Opry appearances
26	January 1975	30	Guitar tunes

Interviews with DeFord Bailey, by Telephone from Dallas to Nashville

30-minute tapes

TAPE NUMBER	DATE
T-1	May 1979
T-2	June 1979
T-3	July 1979
T-4	July–August 1979
T-5	August 1979
T-6	September 1979
T-7	September–October 1979
T-8	October 1979
T-9	October 1979
T-10	November 1979
T-11	November 1979
T-12	November–December 1979
T-13	December 1979
T-14	January 1980
T-15	January 1980
T-16	February 1980
T-17	February 1980
T-18	March 1980
T-19	March 1980
T-20	March–April 1980

60-minute tapes

TAPE NUMBER	DATE
T-21	April 1980
T-22	April 1980
T-23	May 1980
T-24	May 1980
T-25	July 1980

T-26	July 1980
T-27	August–September 1980
T-28	September–October 1980
T-29	October–November 1980
T-30	December 1980
T-31	Undated
T-32	Undated
T-33	Undated
T-34	Undated
T-35	Undated

Personal Interviews with Associates and Friends

Jud Collins (WSM announcer, executive), October 16, 1973, Nashville.

Herman Crook (Grand Ole Opry musician), December 1973, Nashville

Alcyone Bate Beasley (Grand Ole Opry musician), December 1973, Nashville.

Sam McGee and Howard Forrester (Grand Ole Opry musicians), December 1973, Nashville.

Beecher Kirby and Roy Acuff (Grand Ole Opry musicians), 1973, Nashville.

Sam McGee (Grand Ole Opry musician), April 5, 1973, Franklin.

Howard Redmond and Willis Patton, November 3, 1973, Thompson's Station.

Kirk McGee (Grand Ole Opry musician), 1973, Franklin.

G. Miller Watkins (WOAD employee), undated, Nashville.

Bill Monroe (Grand Ole Opry musician), June 23, 1983, Nashville.

Additional Sources

Chapter 1

In the June 24, 1983, issue of *The Tennessean,* reporter Robert K. Oermann gave a detailed account of the activities on DeFord Bailey Day in Nashville that was useful in the preparation of this chapter. A review of a tape provided to the author by NBC television reporter Kenley Jones was also of assistance.

Chapter 2

Material on the Bailey genealogy has been derived from various census records at the Tennessee State Library for Smith and Wilson counties, 1890, 1900, and

1910, and from microfilmed slave records for Wilson County, District Twelve (August 1860), p. 594.

Thomas Talley's *Negro Folk Rhymes* (New York: McMillan, 1922) has been revised, reedited, and expanded by Charles Wolfe and will appear in a new edition from the University of Tennessee Press in 1991.

Information about Henry Thomas and his use of the quills comes from the extensive liner notes by Mack McCormick to *Henry Thomas,* Herwin LP 209. The quotation from DeFord about his use of bones is taken from Bengt Olsson's article, "The Grand Ole Opry's DeFord Bailey," *Living Blues* 21 (May–June 1975): 13-15.

Darlene Gray helped search census records and provided key information about the Bailey family.

Chapter 3

One of the quotations about Bailey's youth has been taken from Bengt Olsson's "The Grand Ole Opry's DeFord Bailey." Some general material on black string-bands comes from Paul Oliver, *The Story of the Blues* (Philadelphia: Chilton, 1970), with material on such bands in Middle Tennessee from the files and research of Charles Wolfe.

Background material on the harmonica and its development has been drawn from various reference works, including *The Grove Dictionary of Musical Instruments,* ed. Stanley Sadie (New York: Grove's Dictionaries of Music, Inc., 1984), and Alan Schackner's *Everything You Always Wanted to Know about the Blues Harp and Marine Band* (New York: Warner, 1975). Some of the older catalogs consulted, including the *Musical Instruments* catalog of J. R. Holcomb (Cleveland, 1889), are in the archives of the Center for Popular Music at Middle Tennessee State University. Additional material has been taken from Michael S. Licht, "Harmonica Magic: Virtuoso Display in American Folk Music," *Ethnomusicology* 24 (1980): 211-21.

Statistics on early Tennessee education come from Lester C. Lamon, *Blacks in Tennessee 1791-1970* (Knoxville: University of Tennessee Press, 1981), 68-70. Data on the 1918 flu epidemic comes from Calvin D. Linton, *American Headlines Year by Year* (Nashville: Thomas Nelson, 1985).

Chapter 4

Information on the T.O.B.A. circuit is found in Oliver, *Story of the Blues,* and the files of the Hatch Show Print Company of Nashville (on microfilm at the Country

Music Foundation Archives in Nashville). Lists of Bijou performers were made available by researcher Doug Seroff.

Information about the recordings of the Bijou artists is found in Robert M. W. Dixon and John Godrich, *Blues and Gospel Records 1902-1943* (Chigwell, U.K.: Storyville, 1982), the definitive prewar blues discography.

Chapter 5

Information on early radio in general is found in Charles Wolfe, "Radio Days," in *Country: The Music and the Musicians* (New York: Abbeville, 1988). Information on early Nashville radio comes from Wolfe's *Grand Ole Opry, The Early Years, 1925-1935* (London: Old Time Music, 1975) and *Tennessee Strings* (Knoxville: University of Tennessee Press, 1976). Also useful is Powell Stamper's company history, *The National Life Story* (New York: Appleton-Century-Crofts, 1968). Some of George Hay's details come from his *A Story of the Grand Ole Opry* (Nashville: privately printed, 1945).

Chapter 6

Information about Henry Whitter comes from research files of Charles Wolfe, and from an article about him by Norm Cohen in Bill Malone and Judith McCulloh, eds., *Stars of Country Music* (Champaign-Urbana: University of Illinois Press, 1975).

Details of the Victor 1928 recording session in Nashville comes from the files of Charles Wolfe as well as microfilm copies of the original Victor session sheets on file at the Country Music Foundation archives. Many of these early recordings, including DeFord's "John Henry," can be heard on the RCA LP set *Sixty Years of the Grand Ole Opry* (CPL2-9507). A complete LP reissue of all of DeFord's 1927-1928 recordings is a British LP called *Harmonica Showcase, 1927-31* (Matchbox MSE 218). This contains all of his released commercial recordings from 1927 to 1928. "Muscle Shoals Blues" and "Pan American Blues," in their 1928 versions, are heard on *Nashville: The Early String Bands*, Vol. 2 (County 542).

Information on Bailey copyrights on file at the U.S. Copyright office was provided by Kip Lornell.

Chapter 7

Paul Oliver's comments about song histories appear on his liner notes to the British LP *Harmonica Showcase, 1927-31*. Information about pop song histories is taken from Joel Whitburn, *Pop Memories, 1890-1954* (Menomonee Falls, Wis.: Record Research, 1986), a compilation of all the major hit records from these years.

Jim Jackson's original version of "Kansas City Blues," as well as information about him, are found in a Netherlands LP entitled *Jim Jackson: Kansas City Blues* (Agram AB 2004). Papa Charley Jackson's basic recordings are heard on *Papa Charley Jackson, 1924-27* (Yazoo LP L-1029). Yet another popular 1920s blues singer, J. T. "Funny Paper" Smith, had a big hit with "Howling Wolf Blues," but neither his original version nor a follow-up sequel resembles DeFord's in lyric content.

W. C. Handy's comments about the "Fox Chase" he heard as a child come from his book *Father of the Blues: An Autobiography* (London: Sidgwick, 1941). References to the Irish analogues to the piece come from Eric Thacker's "Chasing the Fox Chase," *Jazz and Blues* 3, no. 2 (May 1973): 4-5. Other data comes from Michael S. Licht, "Harmonica Magic."

Chapter 8

Background on the early music and radio scene in Knoxville is drawn from Charles Wolfe, "Early Country Music in Knoxville," *Old Time Music* 12 (1974): 19-31; and Willie J. Smyth, "Early Knoxville Radio (1921-41): WNOX and the Midday Merry-Go-Round," *JEMF Quarterly* 28, no. 67-68 (Fall-Winter 1982): 109-15.

Chapter 9

The story about the Delmores paying DeFord a percentage of the gate is found in Alton Delmore, *Truth Is Stranger than Publicity,* ed. Charles Wolfe (Nashville: Country Music Foundation Press, 1976).

Chapter 10

Material in this chapter is drawn from oral interviews listed above and discussions with Bailey family members.

Chapter 11

The outline of the BMI–ASCAP feud is found in a number of standard pop music histories, such as Charles Hamm, *Yesterdays: Popular Music in America* (New York: Norton, 1979). Much of the detail and many of the quotations in this account, though, are taken from a scrapbook compiled in 1941 by Charles W. McMillan entitled "Music War" in the archives of the Center for Popular Music at Middle Tennessee State University at Murfreesboro. The first published linkage of the BMI–ASCAP feud to DeFord's departure from the Opry was detailed in the author's article "Every Day's Been Sunday" in Nashville!, March 1974.

Chapter 12

Information about the tours with WLAC radio star Carl Tipton comes from an interview by Charles Wolfe with Mrs. Carl (Sophie) Tipton, Murfreesboro, Tennessee, February 22, 1990.

Chapter 13

Material in this chapter is drawn from oral interviews listed above.

Chapter 14

Material for this section has been taken from interviews by Charles Wolfe with John Hartford (Nashville, March 13, 1990), James Talley (Nashville, March 11, 1990), Richard Hulan (Nashville, July 20, 1973), and Joe Wilson (Washington, D.C., March 12, 1990). The quotation from DeFord about his house is from Paul Hemphill, *The Nashville Sound* (New York: Simon and Schuster, 1970). Information about the Cortelia Clark incident comes from Frye Gaillard, *Race, Rock and Religion* (Charlotte, N.C.: Eastwoods Press, 1982). An excellent portrait of DeFord during this time is Peter Guralnick's "Pan American Blues" in *Lost Highway: Journeys and Arrivals of American Musicians* (Boston: Godine, 1979).

Details of the 1974 Opry reunion broadcast are taken from a tape recording of the event in the files of Charles Wolfe.

Chapter 15

Material in this chapter is drawn from oral interviews listed above.

Discography

Compiled by Charles Wolfe

This is a list of commercial recordings only, though a number of informal concert and field recordings of DeFord Bailey are known to exist. Each session is followed by the master number of the recording assigned by the company, the title as it appears on the original disc, and the release number (or catalog number) of the original 78 rpm issue, followed by LP or CD reissue album number.

Columbia Phonograph Company: Atlanta, April 1, 1927

143846-2	Pan-American Express	Unissued
143847-2	Hesitation Mama	Unissued

Brunswick-Balke-Collender Company: New York, April 18, 1927

E-22475	Pan American Blues	Brunswick 146, Vocalion 5180
		LP: County 542, Matchbox
		MSE 218

Brunswick-Balke-Collender Company: New York, April 19, 1927

E-22501/02	Dixie Flyer Blues	Brunswick 146, Vocalion 5180
		LP: Matchbox MSE 218
E-22503/04	Up Country Blues	Brunswick 147,
		Brunswick 434
		LP: Matchbox MSE 218
E-22505/06	Evening Prayer Blues	Brunswick 148, Vocalion 5147
		LP: Matchbox MSE 218
E-22507/08	Muscle Shoals Blues	Brunswick 147,
		Brunswick 434
		LP: County 542,
		Matchbox MSE 218
E-22509/10	Old Hen Cackle	Vocalion 5190
		LP: Matchbox MSE 218

| E-22511 | Alcoholic Blues | Brunswick 148, Vocalion 5147 LP: Matchbox MSE 218 Vocalion 5190 |
| E-22512 | Fox Chase | LP: Matchbox MSE 218 |

Victor Recording Company: Nashville, October 2, 1928

47110-2	Lost John	Unissued
47111-2	John Henry	Victor 23336, Victor 23831 LP: Herwin 201, RCA CPL2-9507, Matchbox MSE 218 CD: RCA 6864-2-RDJ
47112-1	Ice Water Blues	Victor 38011, Bluebird 85447, Sunrise 3228, Montgomery Ward M-4910 LP: Matchbox MSE 218
47113-2	Kansas City Blues	Unissued
47114-2	Casey Jones	Unissued
47115-2	Wood Street Blues	Unissued
47116-1	Davidson County Blues	Victor 38014, Bluebird 5447, Sunrise 3228, Montgomery Ward M-4910 LP: Matchbox MSE 218, Yazoo 1053
47117-2	Nashville Blues	Unissued

Note: Reverse of Victor 23336 is Noah Lewis, "Like I Want to Be"; reverse of Victor 23831 is D. H. Bilbro, "Chester Blues."

Index